Reading for Life

14609-DAVI

Reading for Life

100 Christian College Teachers
Reflect on the Books That Shaped
Their Lives

JEFFRY DAVIS, LELAND RYKEN,

THOMAS MARTIN

To order additional copies of this book, contact:
Xlibris Corporation
1-888-795-4274
www.Xlibris.com
Orders@Xlibris.com

Contents

The Teachers and Their Books   23

Dedicated to our students . . .
May you read well to live well

Acknowledgements

Few books come to fruition without the help of many hands. We offer our gratitude to the following teaching assistants for their time and effort as they worked on this long project: Jennifer Karrer, Robert Gormley, and Daniel Driver. We also extend our appreciation to Ruth Davis and David Wright for their many suggestions and valuable design input. Our admiration goes to Stephanie Carter for her exceptional cover artwork; you may contact her at Stephanie Carter Illustration Ltd., *steph@stephaniecarter.com*, toll free 888-730-7080. And most important, we are grateful to the teachers who decided to become contributors—without you this book never would have emerged. To all (and anyone we may have forgotten) we offer our thanks.

To the Reader

As editors, we gratefully appreciate all of the cooperation by the individual teachers of Wheaton College who participated in this three-year project. Each teacher's contribution was the result of a personal choice. No official sponsorship for this book has come from Wheaton College, nor has the College profited financially from the production of this book. Likewise, none of the views or book endorsements should be perceived to be representative of Wheaton College or the faculty as a whole. All errors and omissions are strictly the responsibility of the editors.

Introduction

> "By wisdom the Lord laid the earth's foundations, by understanding he set the heavens in place; by his knowledge the deeps were divided, and the clouds let drop the dew."
>
> Proverbs 3:19-20

A lasting commitment to learning ought to mark the student who graduates from a Christian liberal arts college. For such a believer, entering college as a serious student is second in importance to leaving college as a curious student. "Commencement" means the beginning of one's education–*not* the end. Since God designed and constructed the universe according to knowledge, understanding, and wisdom–the very pursuits of a liberal arts student–graduates face endless possibilities for inquisitive exploration and discovery. Studying the many facets of creation, including human life and culture, can both enhance the graduate's reverence for the Creator and promote a healthy circumspection and humility. This book is intended especially for Christian college graduates who have caught the liberal arts vision for lifelong learning.

A liberal arts education, above all, presumes to teach students *how* to learn, not just *what* to learn. And if students are to continue learning beyond college, one of the most important *hows* they must possess is the skill of reading well. As the ancients understood, reading well demands much more than running one's eyes across a page. Quintilian, the first-century teacher and proponent of the *artes liberales*, emphasized that *lectio*–reading–involved well-developed habits. He writes in Book X of the *Institutio oratoria*, "None but the best authors must be read, and such as are least likely to mislead him who trusts them; but they must be read with attention, and indeed with almost as much care as if we were transcribing them." How does one know which authors are better than others? Teachers–fellow travelers–have long been helpful guides. *Reading for Life* offers personal guidance from those who have perhaps journeyed down roads less traveled, ones worth seeing and experiencing.

Choosing to read worthwhile books with critical care requires not only discrimination, but also personal commitment and discipline. As two more recent advocates of liberal arts learning, Mortimer J. Adler and Charles Van Doren, stress, "good books" are only as good as the habits you develop when reading them. In *How to Read a Book: A Classic Guide to Intelligent Reading*, the authors explain, "Good books are over your head; they would not be good for you if they were not. And books that are over your head weary you unless you reach up to them and pull yourself up to their level." To read well, as Adler and Van Doren encourage, you must "reach up" and "pull." But once that effort has been put forth, the challenges of reading can pay rich dividends.

For those who live their lives according to the Bible, reading well matters. Christians should have an obvious, supernatural interest in the skill, cultivating both the discipline of regular reading and the practice of careful reading. Although reading God's revealed Word remains distinct from other forms of reading, even so, the regular reading of Scripture predisposes us to affirm the importance of written words and their power to influence the way we go about our daily lives. Being the people of "the Book," Christians have good reasons to promote literacy and the kind of learning that comes from reading worthy authors and worthwhile books.

Not long after this book project began, we received an email from a hard-working student who was preparing herself for the inevitable . . . graduation. In her last semester of classes, she realized that soon she would not be *required* to read any more books, as she had for her courses during her four years of study. Yet, as she explained, reading books had profoundly shaped her thinking and personal development. Now, more than ever, she valued the habit of reading good books, a discipline she had acquired in college. Therefore, she intended to continue reading throughout her life, and she wanted some advice from several of her former teachers on how to best accomplish her goal.

This student did not ask for a reading list that recommended current bestsellers or recognized great books of the Western canon; she could get those sorts of lists from various places, such as *The New York Times* or The Great Books Foundation. Rather, she expressed interest in learning about the books that had been particularly significant to us—her Christian liberal arts teachers across the disciplines. Which works did we find most important in *our* development? She trusted us, and out of that trust she wished to encounter some of the very ideas and perspectives from the books that had influenced our thinking and understanding of the world.

Personal direction was what this student desired, and the tone of her email sounded both urgent and hopeful. She expressed a certain confidence that her teachers truly had something to offer her and her friends. Ready to take responsibility for her own travels on the path to life learning, she wanted a little guidance, a map from others to point her in the right direction.

After reading this former student's email, we felt it confirmed the necessity and value of our project: to provide Christian college graduates and other lifelong learners in the church with a collection of significant books, in this case, books that have been formative in the lives of over one hundred Christian college teachers.

Reading for Life has been designed with several purposes in mind, as its title implies.

First, *Reading for Life* provides a glimpse into the books that have been especially influential to the contributors at specific points in their lives. The primary aim of this book, then, is to demonstrate the importance that particular works play in the development of a life—in this case, the life of a thinking Christian, one who attempts to engage the world. Simply put, this is a book of stories in which the contributors talk about the books that have changed their lives, so much so that they would find it difficult to conceive of their lives apart from the influence made by these books.

In addition, *Reading for Life* is a resource that presents its readers with a collection of meaningful writings, representing a variety of genres, disciplines, and perspectives. Consequently, this book's secondary purpose is to direct its readers toward various authors whose perspectives have challenged and transformed the lives of other Christians, namely, the contributors. Although our book is not primarily a reading list, nor is it a list of books that represents a coordinated program of purposeful reading, the collected works here certainly are worth reading; the contributors obviously testify to this. After pondering the many entries, you may find yourself particularly interested in a select number of them because of the way those contributors described their books and their responses to them. In this way, our book provides serious readers with a plethora of tantalizing titles, making up a shelf full of reading for life.

How is this book set up? The approach is actually very simple. We invited the faculty at Wheaton College to choose from one to three books (besides the Bible) that have made an impact upon their lives; the works could be Christian or secular. Then we asked contributors to write a single reflective paragraph of review and commentary for each selected reading. The teachers' choices did not need to relate to their own disciplines; in fact, we encouraged faculty to be cross-disciplinary, opting for readings that truly have had an *influence* on them, either professionally or personally. The result is a good mix of academic and non-academic offerings; some are well-recognized classics of the literary canon, and others are not. Our only caveat to the contributors was that they were to choose works that they believed would be meaningful and relevant (in other words, not too technical or obscure) to an audience defined as "thinking Christians."

The response to our call for contributions was positive. In fact, several contributors expressed great enthusiasm for the project, believing that graduates would really benefit from a guide like this. At the same time, others lamented not having such a book when they graduated from college.

The matter of "trust" became particularly significant to us as we thought about the usefulness of our project, especially in light of technological advancements that make the proliferation of texts both possible and problematic. In the twenty-first century, books are truly ubiquitous; they catch our eyes in expected and unexpected places, from the predictable library or bookstore, to the less expected grocery checkout line or roadstop gas station. This poses a challenge for many thoughtful readers. When considering the millions of titles and the billions of pages of print, where does one begin reading? Moreover, with the astounding daily rate of hypertext production, including ebooks in various genres and an increasing number of books online, how does one determine what is worth the time and what is not? Four hundred years ago, the English scholar and statesman Francis Bacon, who was a voracious reader, could make the claim that "I have taken all knowledge as my province"; however, today such a claim would be impossible. In fact, reading everything in a specialized field presents a difficulty for many learned readers. Consequently, now more than ever, seeking some sort of guidance for reading becomes paramount.

Reading for Life offers assistance to readers in two ways. First, it provides a succinct review of each work mentioned, presenting helpful information so that a potential reader can consider its content. And second, it provides a degree of personal reflection on how a given work has been meaningful to the teacher who presents it. This combination of practical summary and individual response allows prospective readers to make their own informed judgments about what to choose at the public library or the local bookstore.

Also, readers of this guide will see that some of the same books are chosen by more than one contributor. We actually welcomed the repetition of book choices, not asking a contributor to choose a different work if it happened to be selected already by another contributor. The reason for the duplication of titles is simple: we thought it a good way to let our readers know that the more a book has been chosen, the more it warrants serious consideration for future reading.

Our hope is that this book will inspire readers to read significantly, to read more books that have the potential to shape their lives in constructive ways. After considering the contributors and the books that have influenced their lives, readers will recognize how books can promote a heightened awareness of self, of people, of God, of nature, and of the physical universe. Good books can raise questions to readers, as well, causing them to consider new ways of thinking about problems and possibilities. Likewise, readers can ask questions of good books, thereby sharpening their awareness of human experience, expanding their knowledge of the world, and deepening their understanding of spiritual experience. At the heart of a genuine question is the opportunity for an authentic quest. We trust that this book will direct you in your own quest to know, to understand, and to appreciate. To that end, we offer you *Reading for Life*.

Jeffry Davis
Leland Ryken
Thomas Martin

THE TEACHERS AND THEIR BOOKS

Hank Allen,
Sociology

Models of My Life
by Herbert A. Simon

On February 9, 2001, I received a sad message from Carnegie Mellon University announcing the death of Herbert A. Simon, the 1978 Nobel Laureate in Economics. The book cited above is his autobiography: it describes the root ideas, experiences, and people that had influenced Professor Simon's life. Why then is this book great or relevant? Many of the most esteemed social scientists view Simon as the "Einstein" of the social sciences. His work encompasses major theoretical contributions in the fields of political science, economics, sociology, cognitive psychology, artificial intelligence, and organization science. I know of no intellect in the social sciences that can come close to such a rigorous and robust intellectual legacy. *Models of My Life* presents the human side of Herb Simon, showing his many mathematical curiosities, his loyalty to regular friends, and his passion for science. Weaknesses of character and foolish mistakes are also discussed candidly. Simon was of Jewish ancestry, and as far as I can discern, he was not a believer. Yet, of significance to thoughtful evangelicals, this book speaks of the humility and courage endemic to the life of a great intellect. It creatively delineates Simon's personal and intellectual legacy at the threshold of social scientific inquiry during the twentieth century. One is struck by the awesome simplicity undergirding this brilliant scholar. Simon's life demonstrates that exploring the complexities of human societies is its own unsurpassed reward. In this autobiography, he chronicles the joy of intellect. Thus, I will always treasure his personal correspondence with me in an era of uncertainty in my own academic work.

The Division of Labor in Society
by Emile Durkheim

When I think of the simultaneous complexities of ethnic populations, urbanization, educational systems, organizations, and occupations, Durkheim's book stands alone in delineating what I think is the central structural (supra-individual) issue in society: the division of labor. Durkheim, though avowedly secular and naturalistic in his own presuppositions, recognized that the shared morality of collectivities makes any society possible. He accurately discerned that the social ties encapsulating morality shape the collective conscience of society. Embedded in the division of labor, these interdependent social ties are responsible for generating and diffusing culture. Our survival as human beings is predicated upon the division of labor, namely *why*, *when*, *where*, and *how* we work in industries or occupational structures. Our morality is either influenced or governed by the people or groups we work with most closely in this global era. Even the economy rests on a social foundation of trust relations that are the consequence of a common morality. Behind many social problems in church and society, therefore, are the subterranean moral shifts emanating from the division of labor. Thus, struggles over employment, affirmative action, women's rights, crime, poverty, and other public policies are merely recent manifestations of the deeper issues of morality and solidarity that Durkheim studied a century ago. In this book, Durkheim establishes rather conclusively that life in society is not merely a function of individual predilections. Such a truth, I believe, is important for evangelicals to ponder.

Lon Allison,
Christian Formation and Ministry

The Last Battle
from *The Chronicles of Narnia*
by C. S. Lewis

I felt quite silly at first, leafing through children's fairy tales at the age of twenty-two. But as a new Christian, I'd discovered C. S. Lewis from friends who said his *Chronicles* were the best way to befriend the Oxford don. I swallowed the first six books whole, barely taking time to breathe. Then came book number seven–the last one. I dreaded the end, until I discovered that the end was the beginning. *The Last Battle* gave me a glimpse of Heaven, what Lewis calls "The Far Country," and produced in me a longing yet to be filled. No one knows for sure what eternity brings, but my soul is quite convinced I glimpsed something of it in this book. Lewis' images and phrases stir the winds of my spirit. For example, ponder these two lines: "We've got to the country where everything is allowed." *and* "I have come home at last–this is my real country, I belong here." What made the "Far Country" so splendid to me? It was a place of reunion. When I realized that the High King Peter, along with Lucy, Edmund, Lord Digory, and Polly, all "arrive," I reveled in the hope that eternity involves renewed and restored relationships. Truth be told, I still dream, when my guard is down, about lost loved ones. The ache remains. The "Far Country," to Lewis' imagination, was also the end of the old, sad, crumbling, sin-ridden world we now call home. All the good of *this* world is somehow in *that* world, where the blues are truly blue and the greens are really green. It is, as Lewis phrased it, an end to the "Shadowlands." Even to write of it, here, stirs the winds of hope.

Christ and Culture
by H. Richard Niebuhr

Why are there so many kinds of churches? Why do Christians have wildly different views of the role of the church in the world? Niebuhr provides a framework for understanding the differences apparent in these questions. I discovered the differences could fit in five quite distinct categories. I also discovered the differences of opinion or "worldview" driving me mad were historical as well as contemporary in nature. Niebuhr viewed the differences as the way the Church defines and responds to culture. He labeled the categories as 1) Christ Against Culture (the separatist view), 2) The Christ of Culture (the participation view), 3) Christ Above Culture (the synthesis view), 4) Christ and Culture in Paradox (the dualist view), and 5) Christ, the Transformer of Culture (the conversionist view). I saw some of my opinions and views in all the descriptions, but even more, it struck me that all the views might somehow represent the "whole counsel of God." The image of the whole body as necessary, with all its incumbent parts, took shape with Niebuhr's approach. Essentially, his book helped me to find where I most naturally land in my attitude toward the world, and I repented over my lack of patience with believers who "just can't see it right."

Windows of the Soul
by Ken Gire

"Windows" has nothing to do with a computer operating system. Gire's book is a guide to spiritual direction for postmodern people. He opens our soul's longing for God through art, music, and stories ranging from Rockwell's "Girl in the Mirror," to the poetry of Tennyson, to the legend of Camelot. The book gave me a breather from our typical evangelical approach to spiritual devotion: "Read two chapters a day and say your prayers. Oh, and by the way, the earlier in the morning you do it, the better, because God is a morning person." God is more imaginative than that, Gire suggests. He speaks through the books of nature, people, and culture. I guess he encouraged me to keep all five senses on alert for God moments. Through the avenues I've mentioned, Gire then turns the pages of Scripture and drives home heart-needed truths with stunning color. Remember when TV first came out in color? My family watched "The Wonderful World of Disney" just to see the opening scene with the castle and Tinkerbell and the colorful fireworks. Gire's book did a bit of that for me. God and life took on a more rich and wondrous shape and color. Open Gire's book, and open the windows of the soul, breathing deeply to discover God's creativity as communicator.

Dean E. Arnold, Anthropology

The Adventure of Living
by Paul Tournier

I first encountered the words of Paul Tournier when I was in college. His book, *The Meaning of Persons*, was read and discussed campus-wide one semester. Up until that time, I was unfamiliar with the approach of the non-fiction writer as one who could pull the reader into his life through personal anecdotes, a sense of place, and a warmth of spirit. Not long after, I discovered Tournier's *The Adventure of Living* in graduate school, where the isolation and loneliness of concentrated study were challenging, and a great deal of intensity was heaped upon a few relationships. I had been devastated by a failed love affair, an experience of being dumped by a woman to whom I had been engaged. Thus, I was skittish about developing any future relationships after that. Struggling with depression and aimlessness, and uncertain about my future direction, I turned to Tournier, who directed me to the sovereignty of God and the "adventure of living." Tournier argues that life is an adventure, but to live adventurously, one must take risks, trusting in the God who is sovereign. Conversely, taking no risks may be safe, and may mean security, but there is no adventure in such a life. Tournier explains further in the following quotation from the book: "Faith is reliance on this invisible sovereignty of God rather than on our own ability to decide what is 'worthwhile.' If Gutenberg had been asked as a boy what worthwhile thing he might do with his life, he would not have known what answer to give. God guided him to the invention of printing. The majority of our finest adventures are like that. We have no true conception of them in advance but are led into them without knowing exactly how. . . . God guides us, despite our uncertainties and our vagueness, even through our failings and mistakes. . . . Only afterwards, as we look back over the way we have come and reconsider certain important moments in our lives in the light of all that has followed them, or when we survey the whole progress of our lives, do we experience the feeling of having been led without knowing it, the feeling that God has mysteriously guided us."

Dakota:
A Spiritual Geography
by Kathleen Norris

"The high plains, the beginning of the desert West, often act as a crucible for those who inhabit them. Like Jacob's angel, the region requires that you wrestle with it before it bestows a blessing. . . . Dakota is a painful reminder of human limits, just as cities and shopping malls are attempts to deny them." This quotation comes from *Dakota*, a book my daughter first introduced me to when my wife and I visited her in the Black Hills of South Dakota, where she worked during the summer of 1996. Our trip to see her brought back vivid images of my youth and memories of the many trips I had made across the seeming limitless prairies of the western part of that state, where shimmering waves of grass stretch endlessly to the horizon. My daughter assured me that Norris' vivid description of

South Dakota and her spiritual pilgrimage would appeal to me. She was right! *Dakota* is billed as a spiritual geography. It indeed takes the reader on a geographical and spiritual journey in both space and time. Norris' descriptions of life on the high plains evoked powerful memories of life and travel during my youth. As a native of a small town in South Dakota, similar to the town about which Norris writes, I was pulled into the book's many connected narratives. Her town has its gossip, its intensity, and its limits. Also, Norris engenders a respect for the prairie weather, with its blizzards, heat, and tornadoes. What I find so powerful about Norris' writing, however, is her juxtaposition of geographical images with her spiritual pilgrimage. I identify deeply with this book because the images help me to link the seemingly disparate experience of my past with the spiritual journey of my adult years. It fosters a yearning for deeper spiritual life, a deeper sense of my own failings and sinfulness, a deeper need to worship God, and a deeper attraction for the liturgy of the ancient church, with its spiritual disciplines. For me, Norris weaves geography with spirituality in a manner that evokes forgotten memories and promotes my ongoing spiritual pilgrimage.

E. Beatrice Batson,
English

The Christian Idea of Education
by Edmund Fuller (Editor)

The Christian Idea of Education is among my most tattered books, with its pages falling apart and edges thumb-worn. Published a little more than thirty years ago, I have read and reread the book so many times that I now believe that its shabby condition represents the crown of its embodied wisdom. The book contains the papers that a group of distinguished Christian thinkers presented at Kent School, Connecticut, in the autumn of 1955. The thinking is on such a high level that any Christian educator may well ponder for years the ideas articulated not only in the papers, but also in the transcripts of discussion. Although there are nine contributors, a coherent purpose runs through the book: to regain or to restate glimpses of what a liberal education could and should be if college communities were Christ-centered and all courses were taught from a Christian perspective. To accomplish the goal is no impossibility, but it requires the best educated, the wisest Christian teachers who hold the firm conviction that everything valuable for the human being and the human mind belongs to those who belong to Christ. Ideally, the entire educational community should demonstrate a faith that is adventurous, inquiring, receptive to new truth, eager for fresh perspective, while at the same time, a faith grounded in scriptural truth. What results from such a community is not the "Christianization" of the curriculum's content, but rather more learned and committed Christian professors shedding all the light they possibly can on the wider and deeper meanings of the subjects they teach. I remember with deep joy what for me was one of the key phrases of *The Christian Idea of Education*: the right kind of Christian faith can flood a liberal education with meaning as light floods a Flemish painting and gives the scene coherence and significance.

Hippolyta's View
by J. A. Bryant, Jr.

For several reasons *Hippolyta's View* has a unique place in my thinking and in my career. It was among the first books to convince me that the Christian dimension of Shakespeare's writings deserved serious attention. Furthermore, Bryant wrote this book at a point in his own career when he had managed to shake off the direction impressed upon him in his early training and to follow his own inclinations. Only a few years ago, he told me that he wrote the work in a remote part of Mexico, far away from universities, university libraries, and, for the most part, English-speaking people. He wanted to express his own convictions in an honest, candid manner: to say something about Shakespeare's view of poetry, a view which Bryant believed derived from a Christian view of life. His position comes through clearly in the first chapter; remaining chapters demonstrate the Christian dimension in selected dramas. To uncover what Shakespeare was discovering in his re-created world in poetry was for Bryant the standard for the Christian scholar. He feared that some Christian scholars knew what they wanted to see and hence knew beforehand what the text was saying and showing, but I do not believe that Bryant committed this error. He attained his own standard, and perhaps without knowing it, he helped other scholars to write from their own convictions, to be direct, and to search the text.

The Vocation of a Teacher: Rhetorical Occasions, 1967-1988
by Wayne C. Booth

Although this book was published late in my teaching career, I found it so stimulating that I wished every teacher, not only English teachers, could read and ponder Booth's ideas. In many respects the book is an enthusiastic celebration of the teaching profession. Without question, Booth's most passionate defense is that of the teaching of English. Booth is convinced of the necessity of teaching English in a scholarly way. In fact, early in the book he raises a startling question; he wonders whether it is an exaggeration to say that the future of our reading-writing-thinking-speaking culture is mainly in the hands of English teachers. However, no teacher is off the hook, for Booth addresses all teachers in various academic disciplines as well as potential teachers and administrators on all levels. Unwilling to separate teachers into the two categories of scholar OR teacher, Booth's struggle with the definition of scholarship is especially compelling. He is persuaded that those who simply sit at their desks "doing their work" are not scholars, but rather self-repeating mechanisms that are attempting to say once again what they already know. In his thinking, a scholar is one who tries to solve a problem or clarify an issue, not for the sake of some practical or personal achievement. Booth never suggests that the teacher/scholar forget about publishing, but persistently pleads for quality work which results from years of critical thought on a problem or idea. True scholars should produce something new! In the final analysis, Booth wants teacher/scholars to remember that they have a profession to celebrate, and all of them should work hard to express its glories.

Jill Peláez Baumgaertner, English

Absalom! Absalom!
by William Faulkner

I first encountered Faulkner in college, in Georgia, in an un-airconditioned dormitory room with crickets already going strong at eight a.m. I read *Absalom! Absalom!* and my life was changed forever. Up to that point literature had been merely a diversion for me. With Faulkner I saw literature's true nature. I began to understand that fiction, well-written, in the hands of genius, was something that really mattered. When the writer was obedient to the work, an individual and very particular perspective could lead to the big questions, the only important questions: Who am I? Where am I? What am I doing here? I switched majors from chemistry to English. My father had apoplexy. He should have seen it coming, however. With a list of old addresses that could belong only to a migrant worker or a military family, I had always yearned for stability: a place of my own. It was in Faulkner that I discovered both my vocation and my place: the world of the imagination expressed in language—words that cohered and unified vision, words that reached beyond themselves to the ineffable. I was not yet a Christian, but literature taught me both to ask the questions only the

Christian faith could ultimately answer in any satisfactory way and, finally, to find my true home, my real place.

Twilight
by Ellie Wiesel

Twilight, by the 1986 Nobel Peace Prize winner Elie Wiesel, is a book that awakened me out of a soporific stupor too common among academicians. I thought before I read it that I knew what the Holocaust was all about. I had read and taught Wiesel's earlier book *Night.* I had seen and taught Resnais' film *Night and Fog,* with the terrifying Nazi newsreel photos of mountains of hair and boots and eyeglasses, and bodies piled on top of bodies. I had read Styron's *Sophie's Choice* and Thomas' *The White Hotel,* and I had grown up with Anne Frank's diaries. I had read Bruno Bettelheim's outraged response to Lina Wertmuller's film *Seven Beauties,* about a man who survives the concentration camp experience by seducing a repulsive female camp commandant. I have known survivors of Auschwitz, and one of my good friends in graduate school was the daughter of Dachau survivors. She told me of how after her birth in New York City, her parents pushed her carriage into the center of a circle of other survivors who then decorated her baby carriage with written prayers because she was the hope for the future—the only hope. Yes, I thought I knew about what happened in Germany, but I really knew nothing at all until I read this book, and I must admit that the truth of this book cannot be "explained." *Twilight* is filled with questions—the last four pages contain over thirty of them—but they are not subject to discussion or analysis. Nor are they merely rhetorical. Raphael, the main character, wonders if he has dreamed his experience, if it is all a figment of his imagination. He wonders if God is his enemy and whether faith makes doubt necessary. Wiesel is asking all of the questions of the twentieth century and earlier and, I think, much later. In this particular story is the story of millions of others—each unique and each universal. Wiesel's focus is on the linked experiences, the shared sufferings, and God's inscrutable silence.

Bruce Ellis Benson, Philosophy

Truth and Method
by Hans-Georg Gadamer

(Translated by Joel Weinsheimer and Donald G. Marshall)

The label "most influential work on philosophical hermeneutics of the past century" might conjure up images of dry-as-dust theory, yet Gadamer's magnum opus is a veritable banquet of practical and enlivening wisdom. Drawing from a lifetime of reflection, Gadamer moves effortlessly from such topics as music and architecture, to ethics and Christian theology, all in an effort to help explain how human understanding works. But Gadamer's text is more than merely descriptive. Not only does he provide a model of how understanding ought to operate; he also provides a way of going beyond the modern assumptions of the autonomous individual and "objective" knowledge. He offers a chastened view of reason with a strong sense of human limitations and a grateful recognition of the role of community and tradition in shaping our thought—yet with a strong conviction of our ability to know truth. One of the great joys I have as a teacher is that of working carefully through this text and observing its life-changing influence on students, who usually come away from Gadamer with a far deeper appreciation of their religious heritage. Since *Truth and Method* is a sizable tome, readers might wish to whet their appetite with some of Gadamer's essays in *Philosophical Hermeneutics* first.

Pensées
by Blaise Pascal
(Translated by A. J. Krailsheimer)

During a period of profligacy, Pascal became acquainted with friends who found his knowledge of probability useful for their gambling. It may well be to such skeptics that Pascal's apologetic was to be addressed, since an important aspect of his thought is the famed "wager argument." But Pascal never finished his text, leaving us instead with a series of jottings which provide a vast array of profound insights. Since these are *pensées* (i.e., "thoughts") rather than a whole text, one can dip into them freely. Pascal's consideration of various arguments for Christianity is valuable, but my own thinking and faith has been much more influenced by his reflections on the relation of the mind and heart. What separates us from animals, says Pascal, is our capacity to reason; yet reason has its limits and is simply unreasonable when it does not admit them. Ultimately, belief in God requires not merely convincing the mind but also the heart, since our hearts can easily lead us astray. Pascal's apology, then, ends up having a remarkably practical tone, one that can profoundly affect our hearts.

Joy in the Morning
by P. G. Wodehouse

Wodehouse once described his writing as a Broadway musical without music. That description sums up rather well all of his ninety plus works—frivolous, utterly lacking in depth, and without any real message at all. I have learned remarkably little of a philosophical, moral, or religious nature from reading P. G. Wodehouse. Yet he is a master of literary style, with an unmatched ability for the witty turn of phrase. In other words, reading Wodehouse is delightful entertainment, amusing in an intelligent but not terribly mentally taxing sort of way. After all, one can't philosophize all the time. In terms of plot, there really isn't much of one. *Joy in the Morning* is my favorite of the many chronicles of the thick-headed Bertie and the brainy Jeeves. But, since it's out of print and all of the Bertie-and-Jeeves stories are pretty much the same, any one will do. In fact, at one point Wodehouse says that he attempted to defy his critics who accused him of having the same plot and simply changing the characters by keeping both plot and characters the same. One doesn't read Wodehouse for what he says but how he says it. And, if one enjoys the English language simply for its beauty and expressiveness, then reading Wodehouse is truly a joy.

Christina Bieber, English

Beloved
by Toni Morrison

Toni Morrison once said that her novels were "about love and how to survive—not to make a living—but how to survive *whole* in a world where we are all of us, in some measure, *victims* of *something*. Each one of us is in some way at some moment a victim and in no position to do anything about it. Some child is always left unpicked up at some moment. In a world like that, how does one remain whole—is it just impossible to do that?" In *Beloved*, Morrison tells the story of a black woman, Sethe, whose experience of the pain of slavery leads her to an emotional enslavement that she feels powerless to overcome. Morrison illustrates what happens when we allow the pain we have suffered to possess us, when we let it lead us to destroy ourselves and to devour others, all in our effort to feel better. The novel insists that only true community can rescue us from the isolation of our pain by *redeeming* the past–not by forgetting or transcending it. This book has meant a great deal to me spiritually because it serves as a cautionary tale against the kind of death to which unredeemed pain inevitably leads.

A Room of One's Own
by Virginia Woolf

Although Virginia Woolf was not a believer, this collection of essays has been of pivotal importance to me as a woman, as a Christian, and as a Christian scholar. Woolf argues that women writers–if they are to create enduring and true work–must not be afraid to write *as* women in an age in which only men's values are considered to be important. Woolf lauded Jane Austen and Emily Brontë for having this courage and integrity, arguing that "they wrote as women write, not as men write. Of all the thousand women who wrote novels then, they alone entirely ignored the perpetual admonitions of the eternal pedagogue–write this, think that." While our contemporary society has increasingly accepted women's voices, it continues to devalue the intellectual and artistic contribution of Christians. So I have taken from these essays encouragement that I should fearlessly write as a Christian, whether I address Christian topics or not, and whether the larger culture accepts my work or not. Otherwise, becoming essentially false, I will forfeit the distinctive contribution that I may be called to make.

Sarah Borden, Philosophy

Pride and Prejudice
by Jane Austin

I am in the habit of reading *Pride and Prejudice* almost every year, sometimes in the middle of the summer or, occasionally, around March, as winter drags on. I love the wit and style of the book, and there are few things as comforting as a beautiful romance with a happy ending. But Austin's novel is also a story about goodness and ideals, and the myriad of ways in which we can sell them both short. The father, Mr. Bennet, is a character whose impatience leads him to marry a woman he does not respect. Charlotte, a skeptic, does not believe that love is possible, and ends up with a marriage that has little to recommend it, except for financial stability. And then there is Lydia, who fails to look beyond the moment, caught up in merely temporary pleasures. Only Elizabeth and her sister Jane continue to look first for what is good and then, secondarily, for what promotes their own interests. And only Elizabeth and Jane gain happiness, for, as Austin suggests, it is only in pursuing goodness that happiness is found. Sometimes in the last days of winter I need the reminder that, like the heroines of *Pride and Prejudice*, we are called to hold fast to the highest ideals and not to settle for anything less. The Christian walk is not, ultimately, a life of *don'ts*, but a great romance, based on the pursuit of the highest goods.

Andrea L. Broomfield, English

Villette
by Charlotte Brontë

The British novelist Charlotte Brontë holds a high position on my list of favorite authors. She is widely known for her 1847 novel, *Jane Eyre*, but her last novel, *Villette*, best represents this artist's extraordinary talents. Written after the deaths of her brother Branwell and her two sisters, Emily and Anne, *Villette* is imbued with the author's own sorrow and loneliness, and its main character, Lucy Snowe, embodies a life philosophy that is partly the product of Brontë's sustained thinking on matters of faith and doubt. After the unexplained loss of her family and financial resources, Lucy Snowe decides to leave England and move to the continental city, Villette, where the main action of the novel transpires. Much of Lucy's narrative concerns her attraction to a devout Catholic professor of letters who is as wary of Protestants as she is of Catholics. As the two work to overcome their most deeply held prejudices of the other's beliefs, many characters in the novel remain intent on destroying their growing understanding and intimacy. As is typical of Brontë's novels, *Villette* is full of gothic suspense, surprise and romance, but the novel's conclusion is less optimistic than that of *Jane Eyre*. Lucy Snowe's story might be sobering, but those who read this novel will find themselves richly rewarded as they grapple with difficult-to-answer questions concerning God's purpose and our ability to endure in spite of the difficulties that life presents us.

Heart of Darkness
by Joseph Conrad

Perhaps the best known of Joseph Conrad's works, *Heart of Darkness* never fails to make me think deeply about human depravity. On its more obvious level, this novella is a scathing attack on European imperial aspirations and exploitation of Africa. But on a deeper level, Conrad pursues the question of whether humans are capable of maintaining self-restraint and discipline when their society's regulations, taboos, and morals are removed. To pass time while waiting for the tide to turn, the narrator recounts to his shipmates his adventures as a steam-boat captain on the Congo, and in particular his journey in search of the elusive, infamous station manager, Mr. Kurtz. When he realizes the futility of trying to convey to his mates what he experienced on this journey, he finally blurts out: "How could you imagine what particular region of the first ages a man's untrammeled feet may take him into by the way of solitude–utter silence, where not warning voice of a kind neighbor can be heard whispering of public opinion? These little things make all the great difference. When they are gone you must fall back upon your own innate strength, upon your own capacity for faithfulness." Kurtz, we learn, had no strength or perhaps even desire, to control his most base impulses. *Heart of Darkness* is particularly worthwhile reading for Christians because it asks us to consider the degree to which our faith and discipline are dependent on the support of fellow believers, the church, and the spiritual leaders who guide us. What happens to our faith if or when such safety nets are taken from us?

David Bruce, Biology

The Wisdom of the Body
by Walter B. Cannon

I first read this classic by Harvard professor Cannon during my first year of graduate school. Originally published in 1932, the book details what was known then about regulatory processes in animals and humans. In it, Dr. Cannon documents the idea of *homeostasis*, the term he coined to describe the state of dynamic constancy characterizing the body and its subsystems. As a Christian and budding scientist, I found Cannon's exposition of the marvels of the "little machines" that run the body to be fascinating, and I could make a connection between the Designer and the design Cannon elaborated upon. Cannon proposed that homeostasis could be observed in social as well as biological systems, asking, "Are there not general principles of stabilization? May not the devices developed in the animal organism for preserving steady states illustrate methods which are used, or which could be used, elsewhere?" During the past thirty-one years as I have taught biology, especially physiology, I have drawn often on Cannon's insights into the remarkable self-regulating machine that is the human body. Towards the end of *The Wisdom of the Body*, Cannon distills the essence of homeostasis: 1) "In an open system, such as our bodies represent, compounded of unstable material and subjected continually to disturbing conditions, constancy is in itself evidence that agencies are acting, or ready to act, to maintain this constancy"; 2) "If a state remains steady it does so because any tendency towards change is automatically met by increased effectiveness of the factor or factors which resist the change"; 3) "The regulating system which determines a homeostatic state may comprise a number of cooperating factors brought into action at the same time or successively"; and 4) "When a factor is known which can shift a homeostatic state in one direction it is reasonable to look for automatic control of that factor, or for a factor or factors having an opposing effect." These principles, enunciated nearly seventy years ago by one of this century's giants of biomedical science, still pertain in the new millennium, guiding and shaping inquiry into "the little machines" comprising living things on this planet.

Being A Christian in Science
by Walter R. Hearn

"Science deals with problems, religion with mysteries, and philosophy with questions." This quotation opens Dr. Hearn's third chapter, "Science As a Christian Calling." He maintains that persons who are Christians can enter science and contribute to it, without accepting the premise of many in science: "what we can see and measure is all there is." *Being A Christian in Science* is a commentary on Hearn's own life as a scientist. For many years he taught biochemistry at Iowa State University, turning out Ph.D. biochemists of high repute, including one Roger Burgus, a Christian who worked with Roger Guillemin on isolating hypothalamic peptides, a feat which later won a Nobel Prize in Physiology for Guillemin and his competitor, Victor Schally. For the past thirty years Walt Hearn has turned his attention to writing about and interpreting science for the layman and scientist alike. He points out that science is *a* way of knowing, but *not the only way* for knowing (quoting Richard Bube). Hearn explains what scientists do, pointing out that the general public probably has a clearer picture of what detectives do than of what scientists do. Regarding his opening statement, if problems are to be solved and mysteries accepted, what about *questions?* "Should I treat this situation as a problem, and try to solve it—or is it a mystery, which I must learn to accept?" Hearn maintains that "serious questions lead serious people to seek satisfying answers, in the form of lasting truth that one can live by or of some provisional truth that one can live *with.*" He discusses questions important to many young

Christians who are contemplating what to do with their lives. "I wonder if being a scientist might conflict with my Christian convictions?" "Is a scientific career an appropriate response to God's call on my life?" In careful, measured prose, Dr. Hearn paints an insider's perspective of what the life of a Christian in the natural sciences is like. *Being a Christian in Science* is packed with sound, practical wisdom from a respected scientist–a perfect introduction to the doing of science that a young potential scientist needs.

The Human Quest
by Richard H. Bube

Subtitled *A New Look at Science and the Christian Faith*, this book by a Stanford Professor of Materials Science and Electrical Engineering addresses those who have rejected the Christian faith without knowing what it means, and those who have rejected science without understanding it. The book is a series of parallels: the meanings of revelation, evidence, and objectivity are all explored as they relate to science and to the Christian faith. As a renowned scientist and a deeply committed Christian, Bube tackles questions that many skeptics and "searchers" have asked: "What would happen to the world and us if God should suddenly 'turn himself off'?" "How does the world work?" "What is man's place in it?" "What are the solutions to its problems?" Profoundly concerned with the interaction between science and Christian faith, especially among university students, Bube forthrightly engages the centuries-old battle between science and Christianity, in a far-reaching discussion of pressing contemporary issues, such as violence and war, racism, situation ethics, the drug culture, birth control, and euthanasia. It is a book that showed me that an evangelical Christian could also be a scholar and could speak to issues of practical significance in one's life. Bube's writing is clear, comprehensive and always rooted in a high view of Scripture. I found it to be an encouraging treatise as I began my career in academia as a scientist-educator.

Andrew Brulle, Education

Scholarship Reconsidered: Priorities of the Professoriate
by Ernest L. Boyer

Scholarship Assessed: Evaluation of the Professoriate
by Charles Glassick, Mary Huber, and Gene Maeroff

After years of indoctrination into the world of higher education, a focus on what activities were valued for promotion and tenure, and significant reinforcement and encouragement from my superiors, I had the opportunity to teach a Sunday school class on the book of Ecclesiastes. I particularly enjoyed Solomon's characterization of all of our human pursuits as a "chasing after the wind." Reflection on this book of Scripture led me to question my efforts at research and publication and to wonder if I was really doing what God would want me to do. Concurrently with this searching, Ernest Boyer published his short work on the priorities of professors and suggested that true scholarship in higher education could really take one of four forms: scholarship of discovery; scholarship of integration; scholarship of application; and scholarship of teaching. All four are necessary to accomplish the whole of the higher education endeavor, yet not all professors are nor should be expected to be equally proficient in each area. Recently, a group of authors completed Boyer's project and published suggestions that delineated how we in higher education might reconsider what we value and how we conduct faculty evaluations. These two works have been very influential for me in forming my thoughts that we, as professors, must learn to value both the impact of scholarly work and the diversity of scholarly work much more than we do currently. Although we typically tend to view researchers who publish prolifically as the best, these short books helped me come to the conclusion that there is much more to what professors should be doing than striving for another publication.

Trey Buchanan, Psychology

A Palpable God
by Reynolds Price

Reynolds Price is an acclaimed Southern novelist and Professor of Literature at Duke University who hones his writing skill by, of all things, translating portions of the New Testament from its original Greek to English. Raised as a believer in the rural South, Price's keen sense of story moved him to complete a literal translation of the Gospel of Mark—a process that convinced him of the astonishing truth of this ancient text, rich in narrative detail and singular in depicting a remarkable life. His transliteration of Mark—jarring, unsettling, yet ultimately transformative in its ability to draw the reader into the world of ancient Palestine—and his accompanying essay on the uniqueness of the Gospel story—gripping in its assertions—feed both the soul and the mind. If reading modern English translations of the Bible ever becomes ordinary or even dull for you, Price's will move you to approach those stories with fresh eyes and an more open imagination.

Freud:
A Life For Our Times
by Peter Gay

As one of the leading architects of twentieth-century culture, Sigmund Freud is a force to be reckoned with. His writings on psychology are, among many Christians, notoriously materialistic, atheistic, and pessimistic in their depiction of human life and experience. If this characterization is even partially true, how was Freud able to have such a pervasive impact on how we–including Christians–understand ourselves and those around us now, almost one hundred years later? The only way of making sense of this puzzle is to look at Freud's own life, his historical context, and his cultural impact. Noted Yale historian Peter Gay crafts a compelling narrative of the life of this founder of psychoanalysis, a psychological and philosophical theory that has changed (for both good and ill, perhaps) how we look at ourselves. At times both courageous and poignant, Gay paints a picture of a man committed to curing his patients, to finding the truth of the human condition, and, eventually, to struggling with the vast implications of his "dangerous idea"–psychoanalysis. While reading this biography is unlikely to make you a follower of Freud or even to encourage you to embrace many of his ideas, it will deepen your appreciation of the triumphs and tragedies of Western culture during the twentieth century, including Sigmund Freud himself.

Gary M. Burge,
Biblical and Theological Studies

The Space Trilogy:
Out of the Silent Planet; Perelandra;
That Hideous Strength
by C. S. Lewis

When I was a graduate student in Britain in the early eighties, I tried to acquaint myself with the British author C. S. Lewis, a thoughtful Christian and writer who provided a winsome (and sometimes whimsical) study of our world. Lewis wrote his *The Space Trilogy* at the close of World War II, and it is clear that he is wrestling with evil at the level of one who has watched German bombers devastate his homeland. Recently I decided to return to those "old books" and reread them to see why they had moved me so deeply almost twenty years ago. The marvelous thing about these books is that Lewis has built a spiritual universe (fictionally) in which the truths about God and reality are present, just under the surface of things. The universe is animated by spiritual realities, and our human existence is simply one dimension of life.

Out of the Silent Planet

As a professor of medieval and Renaissance literature at Oxford and Cambridge, Lewis was intimately familiar with the presumptions of academia, which informs much of the thematic orientation of the trilogy. The first book begins with the adventures of Dr. Ransom, a Cambridge philologist who accidentally finds himself traveling to Mars (called Malacandra) with two deranged professor-scientists (Weston and Devine). The presumption of these men centers on their desire to rule life like gods, and Ransom must interpret their evil intentions and confront them before the innocent people of that ancient world. Here is a planet populated by races astonishingly different from humans–guided by spirit-beings whose goodness (and power) completely shatter Ransom's materialist worldview.

Perelandra

In the second book, Ransom is commissioned to travel to Venus (or Perelandra) where a new, pristine world is being born–and where he witnesses the temptation of Venus' first woman by the "Unman," a professor completely consumed by evil. Here Lewis explores a truly compelling portrait of temptation and rebellion, showing why a decision to oppose God can be twisted into a delectable, enticing choice for freedom. Ransom wrestles with the problem intellectually as he watches the woman slowly succumb–and then decides that mortal combat against his foe is his only option. The philologist fights raw evil with his bare hands in one of the most dramatic scenes Lewis ever penned. When he attacks the Unman he experiences "lawful hatred" for the first time. It is a torrent fueled by divine wrath.

That Hideous Strength

In the final volume, *That Hideous Strength*, Lewis brings his study to Earth. What would happen if social engineering (with hidden, sinister intentions) won the support of intellectuals in England? Here we meet Jane and Mark Studdock, both academics who are religious skeptics. But Mark's academic insecurities and eagerness to please "the powers that be" make him willing to sacrifice any value for a career. And soon he is allied with evil, growing like a menace in the world. Jane is unconvinced about religion but possesses a permeable worldview, inspired no doubt by mysterious spiritual visions. She meets the now-aging Dr. Ransom and soon is allied with the divine powers of the universe that have now descended on the planet to cleanse it of its corruption. We watch as supernatural powers wrestle–and as commonplace people align themselves in battle either for their redemption or their destruction.

Evvy Campbell,
Missions and Intercultural Studies

Oswald Chambers:
Abandoned to God
by David McCasland

Delving into David McCasland's biography of Oswald Chambers was like finding a treasure. My copy of Chamber's daily devotional classic *My Utmost for His Highest* is well-worn. The brief forward, indicating that the readings came from lectures at the Bible Training College in Clapham and night talks at the Y.M.C.A. Huts in Zeitoun, Egypt, intrigued me but left the author shrouded in mystery. McCasland's dogged and masterful research unveiled the fascinating life of Oswald Chambers. Learning of Chambers' life was instructive to me. I was inspired by his wide reading and vigorous approach to study, his awareness of the eternal stakes during his "dark night of the soul" years, and his spirited engagement with life. I was challenged by the quality of community living in the Bible Training College he established, and I could feel the desert sand in my teeth as Chambers ministered to British soldiers in Egypt during the First World War. The most fascinating thing to me, however, was learning that Oswald Chambers' beloved wife, affectionately known as "Biddy," was a skilled stenographer who recorded her husband's talks verbatim. After Oswald's seemingly untimely death in Egypt, at the age of forty-three, she devoted her life to writing some twenty-five books in his name. I have been challenged by

McCasland's book, which vividly presents the lives of Oswald and Biddy Chambers, a couple who gave their utmost for His highest.

Little Women
by Louisa May Alcott

As a child, my favorite book was Louisa May Alcott's *Little Women*. I was endlessly interested in the lives of Meg, Jo, Amy, and Beth, and I never tired of reading their adventures. The chapter titles reflect Alcott's love of John Bunyan's *Pilgrim's Progress*: "Playing Pilgrims," "Beth Finds the Palace Beautiful," "Amy's Valley of Humiliation," "Jo Meets Apollyon," and "The Valley of the Shadow." The March sisters acted out the drama of *Pilgrim's Progress*. They traveled from the cellar–the City of Destruction–with hats, sticks, and piece bags tied on their backs for burdens, climbing up to the flat housetop where they "stood and sung for joy up there in the sunshine," as Beth described it, basking in the light of their Celestial City. As an adult I find myself going back to *Little Women* for "a bit of a read," reveling in Joe's domestic agony of salted strawberries served with soured cream. I still feel with Meg and servant Hannah that "something better than sunshine brightened the quiet rooms" as they anticipated the return of Mrs. March during Beth's grave illness. Domestic happiness is an enormous treasure in life: Alcott describes that treasure, and the security it brings, with a deft touch that draws one over the years to reread her work.

Sally Schwer Canning, Psychology

The City of Joy
by Dominique Lapierre

When I was assigned to travel to India by the agency I worked for, I was given a copy of Dominique LaPierre's *The City of Joy* in preparation. At twenty-five years old, a middle-class suburban upbringing had done little to prepare me for the degree of poverty I would encounter in Calcutta. The captivating story of Anand Nagar (literally "city of joy") describes with gritty clarity life in one of the poorest, most densely populated sections of this teeming city. It is a story of three men: Stephan Kovalski, a Polish Catholic priest; Max, the American doctor; and the extraordinary Hasari Pal, forced by crippling drought to leave his village and family for the prospect of work in the city. As was true of my experience of India herself, the characters in this book got inside me and stayed there, like the haze of incense. I was thrown off kilter by the jarring juxtaposition of joy and staggering human suffering. Their story destroyed youthful illusions I held of simple causes and solutions to poverty. Instead, the choices facing those in poverty, as well as those who seek to provide some relief to their condition, appear achingly complex. While we recoil in repugnance from the image of human-drawn rickshaw, Hasari Pal finds his salvation in just such a rickshaw: "That carriage, lined up against the pavement, was a gift of the gods," he was to say, "an urban plow with which to make my sweat bear fruit and provide food for my children and for all my relatives waiting expectantly in the village." Much like Frank McCourt in the extraordinary biography *Angela's Ashes*, Pal's resilience is remarkable.

If it is possible for an author to enable his reader to love the one whose story he tells, then LaPierre achieves this. Certainly, God used this human drama of operatic proportions in my life to convey something of His deep love for the suffering and broken of our world.

The Divine Comedy
by Dante Alighieri

Like many students at respectable liberal arts colleges, I was assigned to read Dante's classic trilogy. Everything about the books astounded me, beginning with the subject matter itself. My previous contemplation of heaven and hell paled like wraiths before the richly populated worlds Dante conjures. His vision of the afterlife for condemned sinners includes eternal re-experiencing of the logical consequences of one's earthy sin. This adept and chilling portrayal of the hellish underside of sin helped make real to me, as a young believer, the inherent destructive nature of sins which could appear harmless and pleasurable. Most remarkable is the scope of historical, theological, philosophical, and literary material Dante's project synthesizes. His exhibition of the streams of knowledge available at the time did more to convince me of the value of a liberal arts education than any of the well formed arguments of my professors. It also left me with an abiding sense of humility in the face of the exploding scope of knowledge in our modern world. Finally, I have remained struck by the nagging disappointment I felt at the climax of *The Divine Comedy*. At the time it was disconcerting to reluctantly admit I had been captured more powerfully by the images of hell than his vision of paradise. The world of *Inferno* struck a passionate chord of recognition in me. In contrast, Dante's attempt to portray the fulfillment of perfection seemed unequal in weight; I felt strangely unsatisfied. I was left wondering at how far the effects of the Fall can be felt–hobbling even our yearning for that which we are created to enjoy, restored union with God.

Tuesday
by David Wiesner

This nearly wordless picture book is a surrealistic adventure story set in a small town "Tuesday evening, around 8:00." A group of frogs on lily pads suddenly becomes airborne, sweeping the reader up with them on a wild ride over the sleeping world of grownup life. The frogs show a delightful range of responses to this unfolding adventure, from reluctance to bemusement to complete abandon. Wiesner's illustrations of the bewildered reactions of the few adult witnesses are also funny and at times touching, revealing more about our adult world than would pages of text. I came upon *Tuesday* in graduate school, late one afternoon while wandering the campus bookstore. I remember plopping down, cross-legged, hidden away in the children's section, losing all sense of time and place as I was transported into *Tuesday's* world. I sat there long after the book was finished, enjoying a glow of pleasure, simplicity and peacefulness. While it would be overstating things to claim this one book shaped my life, reading children's books as an adult has indeed influenced me in important ways. First, picture books can be a respite in a word-saturated world. Despite my love for and dependence upon written and spoken language as a professional psychologist, I need the unique nourishment found in the beauty of color and form without words. There is a kind of rest to be found in pictures and the stories they tell. But this book also reminds me of important truths that children already know—that the world is a place of wonder and adventure in which anything might happen, if only we are in the right place, at the right time, looking with the right eyes. And it reminds me that for all of the meaning and import of the adult roles we carry out in life, for all of the responsibility we shoulder, there is something poignant, almost preposterous, in our ultimate situation. We are so limited, and life is so much bigger, more powerful, and less controllable than we want it to be. Wiesner makes us see beyond the veil of those illusions, but rather than raising our fears in the process, reminds us that this unpredictable life of ours can also be a delightful, even magical, thing.

Randy Carey, Military Science

Customs and Controversies: Intertestamental Jewish Backgrounds of the New Testament
by J. Julius Scott

If you are interested in deepening your understanding of the times and context in which Jesus Christ and the apostles lived, this is an excellent resource for your personal enrichment. The book helped me to better understand the Intertestamental history of the Jewish people and why they reacted the way they did to the message, "Repent, for the kingdom of God is at hand!" Likewise, I came to a fuller understanding of what it meant for the Jews to hear the words "The Messiah has come." Dr. Scott does a masterful job of keeping the concepts simple, yet he skillfully incorporates the most relevant and scholarly information available to give his readers a thorough background regarding the events and groups that influenced the mindset of the Jew and the Gentile during the first century A. D. I was fascinated by the impact that the Old Testament and the Intertestamental period had on the first-century Jews. The beauty of this book is that it makes the vast history of God's people more relevant and significant for any believer who is trying to gain a better understanding of the New Testament. In addition, reading this book is sure to enhance the reader's walk with the Lord.

Stephanie Carroll Carnes, English

Anna Karenina
by Leo Tolstoy

Recently I finished reading *Anna Karenina* for the ninth time, and I am convinced I'll never exhaust it. I read it for the first time during my sophomore year in college, and as soon as I finished reading it, I read it again from beginning to end. In the character of Anna, Tolstoy creates a beautiful, vivacious, doomed, unforgettable heroine. Constrained by society to be faithful to her husband and child, yet capable of soaring love with the dashing young Vronsky, Anna appears to be a tragic figure. However, Tolstoy does not let his readers nurture that romantic idea; instead, he challenges the myth of living a passionate life governed by extreme emotion. As we read the novel, we become uncomfortably aware that Anna has cast herself into the tragic role. But fate does not govern Anna's life; Anna does. Her martyrdom is merely thinly veiled narcissism. In contrast with Anna is her sister-in-law, Dolly. Modern readers often chafe at Dolly's apparent weakness. Compared to Anna, she is quiet, long–suffering, and plain; as her philandering husband says, she is "merely a good mother." But Dolly is the character Tolstoy most admires; her moral compass is rarely wrong. It is precisely Dolly's good mothering that makes her so admirable. Motherhood is painful, difficult, and messy, but mixed with tremendous joy. To Dolly, "these joys were so small that they passed unnoticed, like gold in sand, and at bad moments she could see nothing but the pain, nothing but sand; but there were good moments too when she saw nothing but the joy, nothing but gold." Dolly's life is unglamorous and ordinary, but her faithfulness in everyday duty makes her Tolstoy's ideal. What I have come to realize is that Tolstoy confronts his reader with a radical question through this novel: What if your life were judged, not on a few great acts or accomplishments, but on your countless everyday decisions and actions? To Tolstoy, love is not passion and self-abnegation; it is ordinary attention to duty with practical goals and results. *Anna Karenina* taught me to recognize the power of my everyday actions: power to comfort, encourage, and nurture those around me. Active compassion may not be glamorous, but it is redemptive in my life and, with God's help, in the lives of those around me.

A Room of One's Own
by Virginia Woolf

In *The Canterbury Tales,* Chaucer's Wife of Bath says it is no surprise that histories and legends contain negative depictions of women; after all, men were the authors! "Who painted the lion?" she asks, referring to Aesop's fable of the lion who, after seeing a picture of a man killing a lion, remarked that the picture would have been different had a lion painted it. Centuries after Chaucer, the lion finally got a chance to paint. In A *Room of One's Own,* Virginia Woolf proposes a female literary tradition. She argues that if women are to write, they must have money and rooms of their own. Money ensures autonomy, while a room provides privacy—two necessities women often lacked due to property rights laws and family obligations. "Since freedom and fullness of expression are the essence of art," she says, "such a lack of tradition, such a scarcity and inadequacy of tools, must have told enormously on the writing of women." Can women write? Today the question seems absurd, but Woolf addresses it energetically, identifying genius in Jane Austen and Charlotte Brontë and encouraging the young women around her to write well. Woolf's book is a self-evident argument: she brilliantly uses essay, parody, dialogue, and history to argue that women can, in fact, write. What I love most about her writing is that it possesses grace and wit, all in a conversational style that's readable. Woolf's desire for a female literary tradition is rooted in her admiration of genius, not in any myth of female superiority: "All this pitting of sex against sex, of quality against quality; all this claiming of superiority and imputing of inferiority, belong to the private-school stage of human existence where there are 'sides.'" Giving women the opportunity to write should do more to reconcile the sexes than to alienate them. As influential as *A Room of One's Own* has been, students today often read it as at best an inspirational historical artifact, and at worst, irrelevant. Perhaps Virginia Woolf would have been satisfied by this reaction. Seventy years ago, her ideas seemed radical. Today women are part of the larger literary tradition, as we eagerly read forgotten authors and encourage contemporary female writers. It is a tribute to Virginia Woolf that the lions now paint their own portraits.

Ken Chase,
Communication

The Postmodern Condition
by Jean-François Lyotard

In what is perhaps the most frequently quoted book on postmodernism, Lyotard provides the now famous definition that postmodernism is characterized by "an incredulity toward metanarratives." In a nutshell, Lyotard noticed that humanity in the major developed countries has justified the pursuit of scientific knowledge by stories that encompass the broad history of human development. We have pursued knowledge, for instance, in order to free ourselves from the shackles of tyranny or the ravages of nature. Or, we pursued knowledge in order to become

14609-DAVI

enlightened, to arrive at a new state of consciousness in which we have mastery over our circumstances and harmony with one another. The condition of postmodernity is simply that we no longer really believe these stories. Why have these narratives lost their appeal to the contemporary mind? Although Lyotard's characterization is famous, many who reference his definition give little notice to his detailed ethical and practical analysis of metanarratives. Yet I have found his analysis formative for my celebration of Christian ethical practice. Overall, metanarratives tend to eclipse our capacity to attend to that which does not fit within the plotlines of these grand stories. Thus, a belief or preference that does not fit with the overall story is dismissed as an aberration, as unnecessary, or as dangerous to the overall progress of humanity. Metanarratives, then, can justify a terrifying monitoring of beliefs and practices: conform, or be excluded from the story. The twentieth century has seen several horrifying examples of how grand narratives of human emancipation or progress can lead to the deaths of millions. I notice that historical Christianity itself has been both a victimizer and a victim in the human construction of metanarratives. Although I make regular affirmations of the metanarrative of the Gospel, I see that metanarrative as distinctively different from the human metanarratives of terror. The Christian metanarrative does not eclipse those who differ, but urges us to embrace them. We pray, we love, and we live patiently with others, trusting God to make final determinations of who is inside and outside the Kingdom. Furthermore, I now see the biblical teaching on the Holy Spirit differently. Prior to Lyotard, I wanted my Christian faith to fit neatly within set structures of knowledge and action; I strove to construct a stable worldview. Yet Lyotard alerted me to the unexpected, to the new, to the unconventional. In short, Lyotard's essay prompted me to notice Jesus' teaching on the Holy Spirit: "The wind blows wherever it pleases" (John 3:8 NIV). Neither God's historical plan nor His work in each moment with each person can be put in a box. Through the insights of a controversial French philosopher, I have seen this scriptural truth afresh.

Ethics and Infinity
by Emmanuel Levinas

This short collection of radio interviews is probably the best introduction to Levinas' philosophy of ethics. As a French Jew, Levinas brings to contemporary ethics insight that is at once provocative and familiar. Through years of careful philosophical investigation, Levinas exposes the dimension of human responsibility that permeates all human experience. Unlike other ethicists, who simply advocate responsibility as a suitable course of action, Levinas discovers responsibility at the very core of our existence. At the root of our sense of self, of our consciousness of others and the world around us, we are oriented toward others as a servant is toward the master. This is our perpetual calling. Like a pleasant tune that we cannot get out of our head, we live our lives in regard to the rhythm and the beat of responsibility to the other. Since this responsibility is foundational for the development of human consciousness, then all our daily interpretations and actions are ways of dealing with this fundamental orientation of our being. Levinas' insight has enormous implications for social life and politics. It means that human freedom to do what one wants, or freedom from the intrusion of others, is not the defining moment of human existence. Rather, freedom emerges when we face multiple others calling us to respond and serve. Freedom is not negative, but a positive orientation to the others. Unfortunately, we often think of our social life as organized to keep people from each other. Levinas would urge us to construct a social life providing opportunity to move toward one another. Justice, then, becomes the attempt to serve each person in a dispute, without dismissal. Overall, Levinas' Jewish dependency on the Old Testament shines through his philosophical analysis. He recognizes an ultimate Good underlying all human existence, and his thought encourages us to live in the light of that Good. Most remarkably, he makes this case for the secular mind. Through Levinas, Christians can be challenged to *live* love and justice at the deepest level, and they can also be enabled to build ethical bridges with those who reject Judeo-Christian values.

Robert E. Coleman,
Christian Formation and Ministry

The Pilgrim's Progress
by John Bunyan

Though published in 1678, the book is still available in numerous editions. My first copy, well worn with age, follows the older King James idiom, so I recommend one of the newer versions with more contemporary language. (*The New Pilgrim's Progress, with Notes by Warren W. Wiersbe* is the edition I now read.) This classic dream of the main character—Christian—and his pilgrimage to the celestial city, which has inspired millions of readers, did not really get my attention until graduate school at Princeton. Perhaps it was the simplicity of the allegory that attracted me. It seemed to break through the labyrinth of theological complexity with which I was grappling and spoke with profound eloquence to the real struggles of faith in my walk with Christ. Not surprisingly, the book has become well known in my Theology of Evangelism classes, where it is required reading. I should mention, too, that some years ago the children's version was read in our family devotions around the table at home. Whenever I read the book, I never fail to see something fresh and beautiful to ponder.

Pensées
by Blaise Pascal

Few men have thought more deeply upon the nature of reality than Blaise Pascal. Beginning with the human problem, he shows there would be no meaning, nor purpose, in life apart from God's disclosure of His Word. Indifference of the skeptic is overcome by means of a "wager," whereby everyone is confronted with an all-encompassing choice: either

God *is*, or He *is not*. One who responds in the affirmative has everything to gain and nothing to lose, whereas the person who denies God has nothing permanently to gain and everything to lose. Though it is self-interest that provokes the reasonable decision, still it causes one to move from a habit of disbelief, and invites a new direction toward truth. God's saving revelation, however, comes only through divine illumination in the believer's soul. By this, Pascal does not mean mystical emotion, but rather an intuitive love for God Himself. The focus is Jesus Christ, the object of all Scripture, for He alone incarnated the Infinite Word in our human estate. In His Person is revealed both the Truth of God and the Truth of mankind. Yet only persons who renounce self-love will know what this means. Herein is exposed the error of those who do not find the Truth. A genuine Christian, Pascal points out, does not squabble over signs, but humbly bows in adoration before the Lord. Pascal was still working on the *Pensées* when he died at the age of thirty-nine. Though these fragments of thought never developed into a complete apology, as originally planned, in my opinion they represent one of the most extraordinary insights into human experience ever penned.

Christian Perfection
by Francois de Salignac de La Mothe Fenelon

These essays by the saintly seventeenth-century French Catholic Archbishop have a depth seldom found in literature, certainly as compared to popular contemporary religious writing. Fenelon has little sympathy for those who pamper the flesh, lusting against the Spirit. To him, following Christ is the way of the cross, and he sees implications of that crucified life that are not easy to face. When I stumbled across this book, it startled my anemic dedication. Yet, recognizing my failing, I was made to see greater dimensions of spiritual reality to which my soul aspires. In our postmodern, Western world of self-indulgence, where the church languishes in Laodician mediocrity, this kind of reading is not likely to have appeal. Still, for serious followers of the Christ, it speaks to the deeper yearnings of the soul.

14609-DAVI

Christine Colón, English

The Waves
by Virginia Woolf

"We don't get this!" was the cry that emanated from my classmates and me upon our first reading of Virginia Woolf's *The Waves*. As undergraduates who were frustrated by our first exposure to stream-of-consciousness writing, we felt a bit confused. But after slowly working through the text, we started not only to appreciate the novel but also to recognize how our process of coming together as a group to decipher the text mirrored the ideas that Woolf develops in her book. In *The Waves*, Woolf explores the friendship of six individuals and illustrates the amazingly powerful influence that they have on each other. The fluidity of the narrative, which we had originally found so frustrating, actually illustrates how completely the characters' lives are intertwined. Gradually, our cry of "we don't get this!" was transformed into the mantra "we are the waves." The novel came to symbolize both the struggles we had undergone in the class and the relationships we had forged with each other. Now, each time I read the novel, I am struck by Woolf's ability to convey the extraordinary power that each human being has to influence others. While Woolf approaches the subject from a secular viewpoint, I like to think that, as Christians, we have a duty that is even more important: adding our unique music to the world of friendships that, as Woolf describes, represents a "symphony, with its concord and its discord and its tunes on top and its complicated bass beneath."

Sharon Coolidge, English

Sir Gawain and the Green Knight
by an Anonymous Medieval Writer

I first read the medieval romance *Sir Gawain and the Green Knight* as a high school student and thought it was a nice story about chivalry. But ironically, it was during my graduate study at a secular university that I began to understand the profoundly Christian vision in this work. This short text tells the story of a knight in King Arthur's court who is challenged one New Year's Day to a "Christmas game": a giant green knight invites young Gawain to swing an ax at his head, and if he survives, the green knight gets the opportunity to swing an ax at Gawain's the following year. Gawain thinks he has the upper hand when he accepts the game and takes the first swing; however, the stunned young knight watches as the newly beheaded green knight "resurrects" before him. Gawain then realizes that he will have to receive a stroke from the ax of this magical man twelve months hence, and that he will certainly die. Told through symbols and rich humor, the rest of the story narrates a journey of physical suffering and deceptive ease that is really an unexpected spiritual pilgrimage of redemption. This tale challenges us to confront in new ways what it means to trust God fully, even if it means risking death. Only at the end, when all is revealed, do we (and Gawain) come to understand the true nature of God's mercy and grace in the face of our pride and humiliating finiteness.

The Divine Comedy
by Dante Alighieri

As a senior in college, I first read Dante's *Divine Comedy* and was fascinated by the complexity, vision, and imagination in this amazing work. I read it again as a part of a graduate seminar, this time reading more deeply and carefully but still responding to it as a great intellectual achievement. It wasn't until I started teaching it (sometimes twice a year) that this work really took hold on me and had a profound effect on my own Christian life. It describes in great detail a man's physical journey through hell, purgatory, and paradise, though on a deeper level, it narrates Dante's (and our) spiritual journey from a sinful, fallen condition back to a joyful union with God. As I reread and teach this work each year, what strikes me again and again is the importance of trying to see the world through God's eyes, of not worshiping the things of the world (material goods, power, wealth, even relationships) in the way we live out our lives, but of loving God first with all our being and then using the gifts he gives us in this world to worship and glorify him. This is a work I find rich, complex, and sometimes difficult, but one that is always provocative and rewarding.

Lynn O. Cooper, Communication

The Last Year of the War
by Shirley Nelson

The Apostle Paul used the Greek word *koinonia* thirteen times in the New Testament to denote a community of believers devoted to the teaching of Scripture, fellowship, eating together, and prayer. What would that community look like today? In *The Last Year of the War,* Shirley Nelson chronicles the first semester in the life of a freshman attending a Chicago Bible institute in 1944. In doing so, Nelson focuses a knowing eye on the blessings and burdens of living in Christian community. Through the eyes of a young woman named Jo, we watch a newcomer to the faith as she grapples with issues of identity and belonging, guilt and grace. Jo's attempts to communicate who she is and what she needs are painfully portrayed as she tries to adjust to her new world. The story caused me to confront my own hypocrisy as a believer, as well as my tendency to judge rather than understand others. To anyone who has struggled with relationships, or who has wondered what it's like to live in genuine community—specifically within the milieu of an evangelical Christian campus—I recommend this bittersweet novel.

To Kill a Mockingbird
by Harper Lee

To Kill a Mockingbird was my consciousness-raising book. Coming to age amid the tumult of the Sixties was a marked experience in a country exploding with change. More than the horror of the nightly newscasts about the Vietnam War, or the blast of rock guitars on the radio, or the incoherent claims of drug users, or the protests of civil rights marchers, my catalyst for personal enlightenment came from the still, quiet voice of Harper Lee. Lee gently brings to life the lazy, carefree days of a Southern summer. As she introduces the sensitive character of Jem and his precocious sister, Scout, the reader enters a safe and familiar place that is overseen by the distant but beloved father, Atticus. Atticus is a symbol of strength and civility in a world that, like mine, was quickly changing. The summer I read *To Kill a Mockingbird* mirrored the summer of my "real" education. Like Lee's children, my childlike eyes were opened to a world that is both dangerous and cruel. And as with the child who weakly protests "it's not fair," I learned, with painful recollection, that good intentions and compassion are not always enough, and that justice—in this time and place—does not always prevail.

Jeffry Davis, English

King Lear
by William Shakespeare

My first encounter with this play took place during my senior year at Wheaton, in Dr. Batson's course on Shakespeare. As one newly initiated into the mysteries of the Bard's craft, I reveled in the play's engaging dual-plot structure, its portrayal of familial strife, its pagan and Christian overtones, and its profound message of love and forgiveness. When old Lear decides to give away his kingdom, piece by piece, he rashly misjudges the intentions and character of each of his three daughters. Moved to blind rage by his youngest and most faithful child, Cordelia, Lear refuses to listen to reason. In fact, when his most trustworthy servant, Kent, begs him to "see better" and not punish Cordelia, Lear reaches for his sword, threatening to kill him if he ever sees his face again. From here, the drama unfolds with magnitude, evoking pity and fear by its end—the two essential components of a great tragedy, according to Aristotle. Since my initial reading and consideration of the play, I have gone back to it numerous times, both as a teacher and as a mere reader. And more recently, caring for two ailing parents—one with Alzheimer's disease and the other with cancer—I have found strange comfort from considering King Lear: first, his gradual movement into madness (in many ways not unlike what I have witnessed with my mother); and second, the old man's desperate attempt to maintain control

in the midst of overwhelming circumstances (much as I have seen my
father do in his attempt to care for my mother, and himself). As long as
I live, I will vividly recall Dr. Batson's dramatic reading of the last lines
of the play, especially Lear's repetition of the word "never" five times,
signifying both his resignation in the face of death, and his defiance. As
critic Richard Sewall explains, "Like Job and Oedipus, Lear shows himself
more than sinner, more than sinned against. He does evil, and evil is
done to him; but in the course of his ordeal, which in part he brought
upon himself, he transcends both these categories. Like other heroes,
he ends victor as well as victim."

Quintilian On the Teaching of Speaking and Writing: Translations from Books One, Two, and Ten of the Institutio oratoria
by Quintilian (Edited by James J. Murphy)

Introduced to Quintilian in graduate school, I became so impressed by
the depth of his ethical commitments and educational insights that I
decided to do my dissertation on his approach to writing and his influence
upon select Christian writers. Surprisingly, few educated Christians know
the name of Quintilian, the first-century teacher of reading, writing and
speaking who lived in Rome at the time of the Apostle Paul. Yet, aside
from maintaining an unswerving commitment to moral educational
values during the most decadent period in Roman culture, and aside
from having one of the most profound influences upon the development
of the Western educational system and Christian thinkers throughout
and centuries, Quintilian was probably the first pagan writer to be
influenced by an early Christian convert. Murphy's collection of three
of the most important books from Quintilian's twelve-book work
entitled the *Institutio oratoria* proves to be readable and relevant, especially
for those who advocate character formation as a central part of a child's
development. Book I addresses aspects of early childhood education, at

home and in school. Book II considers the importance of the study of rhetoric by teenage students who intend to become proficient and eloquent in all communication skills. And Book X examines the connection between writing well and reading well. A strong proponent of liberal arts learning, Quintilian would agree with the idea that a "good" student is not merely one who succeeds in school and gets good grades; rather, a good student is one who makes a commitment to become virtuous and to pursue things that are inherently good and worthy of one's time and effort. With great interest, I continue to read Quintilian's ancient wisdom, and I write about his relevance to educators today.

The Road Less Traveled: A New Psychology of Love, Traditional Values and Spiritual Growth
by M. Scott Peck

Given to me by some friends from church, Peck's book helped me to weather the vicissitudes of my twenties. The book's first sentence–"Life is difficult."–has come to mind repeatedly, especially during times of great struggle; it sets the clear and candid tone that carries throughout all four chapters. As a good therapist, Peck attempts to identify and dismantle the destructive shibboleths people tend to live by, offering, in their place, a perspective on living that boldly calls for a courageous adherence to honesty and discipline. For example, Peck writes, "True love is not a feeling by which we are overwhelmed. It is a committed, thoughtful decision." Though at times his words verge on aphoristic oversimplification, Peck does not resist complexity, nor would he chide those who assert life's mystery, as his final chapter on grace reveals. He does, however, believe that mental health results from consistent choices that stem out of principled convictions. Part of Peck's appeal, for me, results from his prophetic voice: much of what he writes challenges common societal attitudes which have become sacrosanct, such as the notion that I should have the right to do whatever I want to do in the name of "freedom," regardless of the consequences. I pick up my worn copy of this text whenever I feel the need to be personally challenged or to face profound relational truths. Peck skillfully shows the folly and frustration of a life devoid of values and ultimate commitments. Yet, although his writing can in some ways be painfully honest to read, I have found that it is always therapeutic, in the best sense of the word.

Lyle Dorsett,
Christian Formation and Ministry

Orthodoxy
by G. K. Chesterton

Orthodoxy is a stunningly brilliant book. Written by one of the literary giants of the early twentieth century, it has a power unlike any other Christian book. For decades, floundering Christians have been strengthened and encouraged by this masterpiece. Likewise, agnostics and seekers of spiritual truth have turned from darkness to the light by reading this compelling apologetic for the Christian faith. I, too, was markedly influenced by this work. After reading it, the scaffolding of philosophical materialism that I stood on was permanently shaken. It was not long afterwards that I became a Christian. One particular theme developed by Chesterton that spoke to me was the condition of always feeling "homesick at home." Chesterton said that after he became a Christian he understood why he had always been "homesick at home." He did not say he ceased being homesick; rather, he realized why he experienced that sensation: this world is not our home.

Paul Egeland,
Education

A Wrinkle in Time
by Madeleine L'Engle

The Murrys first piqued my imagination as a student in a children's literature course at Wheaton College. I connected with many aspects of L'Engle's characters: Meg's awkward adolescence; Sandy's pragmatism; Charles Wallace's vulnerability; the parents' scientific interests; and the optimism of Meg's friend, Calvin. Later, as an elementary school teacher, I encouraged my students to revel in L'Engle's "tesseracts" and time travel. I enjoyed introducing them to this fifth dimension in the context of a confrontation with evil, won by children using whatever loaves and fishes they possessed. Meg's selfless actions to save her father and brother remain as inspiring and memorable sections of the book. What continues to challenge me, however, is L'Engle's handling of ambiguity. Contrary to my natural tendencies, she is not unsettled by tough questions and unpredictability. Early in the book, Mrs. Murry expresses it this way: "I don't understand it any more than you do, but one thing I've learned is that you don't have to understand things for them to be." She also makes me question my inclination toward an objective view of reality. Do I focus on what things *look like* or what they *are like*? *A Wrinkle in Time* is one of those rare books that continues to be enjoyed by both children and adults— and especially this adult.

Amazing Grace:
The Lives of Children
and the Conscience of a Nation
by Jonathan Kozol

For decades, Jonathan Kozol, former public school teacher in Boston, has been raising the awareness—and conscience—of educators and policy makers in the United States regarding the many inequities in education. Following one of Kozol's earlier works, *Savage Inequalities*, this book displays the injustice of our present formulas for funding education, as personalized through the lives of the children in the South Bronx, New York. While initiating a program to bring inner city children to Honey Rock Camp, one of my summer school students graciously shared this book with me. What intrigued my student, and me, was how Kozol was able to find "amazing grace" among the poor, the neglected, and the sick of this impoverished community. Through the voices of the children, their family members, the ministers of St. Anne's Episcopal Church, and some of the teachers in the local schools, the reader can hear and see the reality of violence, anguish, and disease in this community; yet, glimmers of hope exist in a neighborhood that—while foreign to me—proves to be too familiar to many. This book continues to provide a personal benchmark as I reflect on my commission to be part of an educational institution that seeks to serve others for Christ and His Kingdom.

Duane H. Elmer,
Christian Formation and Ministry

The Shantung Compound
by Langdon Gilkey

During World War II, over two thousand Westerners were placed under Japanese control in a "Civilian Internship Center" in Shantung province, about two hundred miles south of Peking. With minimal amenities and living space, and no social structure, this group forged its own society. How do human beings behave when stripped of past vestiges that so neatly defined their lives? Do people act morally when it does not serve their own interests to do so? Upon what foundation are principles of justice established? This book reveals some striking answers to these questions. Greed and sundry rationalizations created strife in this compound that threatened the fragile social fabric of the people within it, who needed internal integrity and interpersonal commitment to survive. Such realities drove the author from his Enlightenment assumptions to believe that only in a God-centeredness can a society transcend the injustices of each human heart. This low-key but gripping drama of life startled me when I first read it. I found myself imperceptibly sliding into a seat of judgment over these often pathetic souls. Then, near the end of the book, I discovered a more disturbing truth: this story, from a time past, dealing with people who seemed unlike me–this was actually a story about me, at my best, and at my worst.

The Spring Wind
by Gladis DePree

Set in post-World War II Hong Kong, this obscure missionary autobiography is acclaimed by many of my students to be the most insightful book they have ever read. And I agree. While those in inter-ethnic or inter-cultural ministry might find the book more immediately relevant, anyone trying to be effective in virtually any context will find it profitable. The theme, never directly stated, involves a view of personhood. In essence, the theme is represented by this question: What does it mean to bear the image of God, especially if one is a non-believer? A second theme addresses an individual's rights as a person and a member in community. With an extraordinary literary style, DePree subtly engages the reader in story until we discover ourselves through the characters presented. Our view of people profoundly determines how we witness, how we give and receive nurture, and how we relate to people who are different from us. It also provides a compass for determining my rights and the exercise of them. DePree's writing has helped me parent, teach, and work with varieties of people. After eight readings of this book, I look forward to the next reading all the more. I will not be disappointed, I am sure.

David B. Fletcher, Philosophy

Three Futuristic Dystopia Novels:

1984
by George Orwell

Brave New World
by Aldous Huxley

Fahrenheit 451
by Ray Bradbury

While no one would have predicted an academic career for me, given my blue-collar Chicago upbringing, I was blessed by an early reading ability, and my life has been shaped from my early years by the many books I have read. Now as a philosophy professor with special interests in ethics, I can trace my moral passion to a number of books, but perhaps the most influential were futuristic novels of dystopia: George Orwell's *1984*, Aldous Huxley's *Brave New World*, and Ray Bradbury's *Fahrenheit 451*. All three of these novels are similar in that they explore the life of an individual coming to self-awareness in a society oppressed by a government that subjugates not necessarily through overt brutality, but through technology and behavior control. The main character in each—whether Orwell's Winston, Huxley's John the Savage, or Bradbury's Montag—discovers and attempts to assert individuality and liberty against peers who are content to live satiated, programmed, yet deeply joyless and meaningless lives. Of particular relevance to my present work in bioethics is *Brave New World*, which, though written seventy years ago, foresaw the uses to which genetic engineering could be put in an increasingly conformist society with a totalitarian government. Through a combination of embryo manipulation and behavioral conditioning, individuals are produced in laboratories to fit into a strict caste system in which Alphas are destined for intelligence and professional careers, while Betas, Gammas, and Deltas are destined for decreasing levels of intelligence and responsibility. Like many others writing in the field of bioethics, I find I am frequently moved to pessimism about our probable abuses of bioethical advances by the grim vision of genetic and behavior-control technology presented in *Brave New World*. Further, as a Christian, I note that in all of these dystopia novels, part of the strategy of control over people is to prevent them from thinking about the ultimate questions of God and faith, because such thoughts can create distress and, ultimately, motivation for change. As John the Savage says in *Brave New World*, "But I don't want comfort. I want God, I want poetry, I want real danger, I want freedom, I want goodness. I want sin." These books remind us that the ultimate questions of faith, meaning, and morality should never be ignored.

Curtis H. Funk,
Conservatory of Music

I Heard the Owl Call My Name
by Margaret Craven

Although the community of my childhood home in Canada was adjacent to a large Indian reservation, I never gave these first nation people a second thought. So it was with some indifference, despite the recommendation of a friend, that I started reading this book about a priest whose parish was the Kwakiutl Indians on the northern coast of British Columbia. Now, several years later, I find myself recalling the words of the text and, even more, the images portrayed in those words. There is a muted quality about this story, a sense of "autumn" at a time and a place removed from our "here and now." It is "autumn" for the Indian village that is witnessing the effects of modernization and the intrusion of Euro-Canadian culture. "When they were seated there was a long silence, as the old watched Mark intently and soberly. It was not the drinking that had brought them here. It was not even the loss of the young. It was something that led back into the deepest beliefs of the tribe." And it is "autumn" for the young minister, Mark Brian, who though dying of cancer, comes face to face with his spiritual calling. "He went to the door and opened it, and he stepped out into the soft white night, the snow whispering now under the footfalls. For the first time he knew them for what they were, the people of his hand and the sheep of his pasture, and he knew how deep was his commitment to them." These words haunted me the first time I read them, as they do even now as I write. And I ask, "Who are the sheep of my pasture and how deep is my commitment to them? How shall I respond when the owl calls my name?"

Balkan Ghosts:
A Journey Through History
by Robert D. Kaplan

This morning, as I write, the radio newscaster reports the burning of the Yugoslav parliament building in Belgrade–another violent episode in the confounding history of the Balkans. Having lived briefly in Romania after the "revolution" of 1989, and having seen the poignant beauty of the region from occasional travels there, I can hardly believe, much less understand, the Gordian knot that represents the history and culture of the Balkan region. Aptly titled, *Balkan Ghosts* is a penetrating look into the dark and lingering cultural "ghosts" of each of the territories. Here are stories seldom told beyond the Balkan borders, an unraveling of a series of complicated and confusing plots that defy comprehension. Kaplan, a journalist, presents the material as a well-informed traveler making his way from city to city throughout the Balkan region. With each stop, the sights, sounds, and characters he encounters act as a springboard for him to probe the mysterious past. We begin to get a picture of a tapestry woven with rich and varied cultural colors against a backdrop of bloody atrocities, religious fanaticism, and tyrannical leaders. Kaplan has written a masterpiece. After reading a library copy of this book, I went out and bought my own and began to read it again.

Music, Society, Education
by Christopher Small

Published first in 1977, this little book–with its benign title–has a powerful and disturbing message: imbedded in the brilliance of Western culture's art and science, as well as the society it both reflects and shapes, is an impoverishment that could be the death-trap of our culture. The author begins his treatise with an elegant description of Western culture since the Enlightenment as embodied in musical art and dominated by scientific methodology. Then, through an insightful look at non-Western practice–both of the arts and of the natural sciences–he hits us with the realization that not all is well in our Cartesian world. It is not only the scientific worldview that "elevates the intellect and exultation of abstract logic." The arts, too, have been complicit in "the enthronement of reason and logic as the highest human functions." The resultant and complementary devaluation of other mental processes, Small suggests, has led our society and our educational institutions into an intellectual cul-de-sac, if not towards a cultural hell. "We have produced a generation who knows more about the world, and experiences it less, than perhaps any generation in human history." Risking controversy, Small offers an alternative view of art that could "serve as a model for a new vision of education, and possibly of society." Now in a reprinting (1996), Small's work is still as challenging, as combative, and as stimulating as it was when it was first written.

Robert L. Gallagher, Missions and Intercultural Studies

The Release of the Spirit
by Watchman Nee

I surrendered my life to the Lord Jesus when I was nineteen years of age in a small Australian Pentecostal church. Those early years were full of great zeal for my new-found faith. I felt I could do anything in the name of Jesus. The Jesus Movement from California had splashed onto our Australian shore, and hundreds of young people found spiritual reality in Christ. And into the center of this triumphalism came a small book of a mere ninety pages that brought me to my knees. As I read *The Release of the Spirit*, I became breathless as Watchman Nee communicated on the importance of brokenness. According to Nee, only through a believer's brokenness can the human spirit release the presence and life of Jesus Christ; thus, this is how we can serve effectively. For God's people to be increasingly fruitful, the Lord needs to be released through a human spirit that is quickened and controlled by the Holy Spirit. Nee explains the necessity of brokenness in the lives of those who desire to be brought under the control of God's Spirit. His vivid presentation of the beautiful alabaster box being broken, with its fragrance filling the house with refreshing delight, has stayed with me for more than thirty years.

Celebration of Discipline: The Path to Spiritual Growth
by Richard J. Foster

It took me a while to understand that effective spiritual ministry flows out of being and not doing. Serving God is not only doing things right, but doing the right things. My shift in ministry from *doingness* to *beingness* stretched out over an eighteen-month period, and included a number of cognitive and experiential transformations. One such significant spiritual dynamic came from encountering Richard Foster's *Celebration of Discipline*. The author describes the classic spiritual disciplines that Christians through the ages have practiced, both individually and corporately, in order to come into the presence of God. As I worked through the earlier chapters on prayer, fasting, study, solitude, and silence, the Holy Spirit challenged me to do what was suggested. So, I learned to delegate things rather than do them myself, to say "no" more often, even to wonderful opportunities, and to carve out time from my over-flowing schedule so that I might "waste time" with Jesus. Foster helped me to see that my theological tradition was a small part of God's involvement with humanity through the centuries of church history—clearly, the Holy Spirit did not stop working after the apostolic times, only to reappear in 1906 at the Azusa Street revival. Best of all, the application of the book to my life provided a platform upon which I could stand to gain a better glimpse of the smiling face of God.

The Making of a Leader: Recognizing the Lessons and Stages of Leadership Development
by J. Robert Clinton

I moved to Pasadena, California, from Australia with my family after twenty years of pastoral ministry. During my first semester at Fuller Theological Seminary, I read Bobby Clinton's *The Making of a Leader*. The principles in the book brought healing to old ministry wounds, fanned the embers of my calling, and gave me hope for the future. Based upon Clinton's study of the lives of hundreds of historical, biblical, and contemporary leaders, the book identifies the patterns and processes that God uses to develop a leader. He suggests six stages of leadership development, and he encourages readers to determine which stage in the process they might locate themselves. As I worked through the book, it was amazing how many processes I had experienced at the particular phases Clinton described. I gained four insights from the book. First, a realization that God's sovereignty was ever present in my life. I sensed God's continuing work in my past to develop me as a leader through tough times, as well as good ones. With this came the assurance that what I had gone through was normal. Also, I received an anticipation of what God was going to do in the future. Finally, these concepts have been helpful as I have worked in the development and training of others, for which I am grateful.

Ruth Givens,
Education

Pilgrim at Tinker Creek
by Annie Dillard

Reading Annie Dillard vitalized my meditation on the human condition and its relation to God. In her *Walden*-like book, she describes an assent into a contemplative encounter with nature: she is not only an observer, but as the title suggests, she is a *pilgrim.* Instead of the passive introspection one might expect, Dillard presents her rough-and-tumble journey to know what it means to be alive in a world that is "wilder . . . more dangerous and bitter, more extravagant and bright" than most of us ever realize. Dillard challenged me, through my imagination, as moths and mosquitoes became microcosms of our frail human existence. Unlike her predecessor, Thoreau, however, Dillard insists on God's participation in life, even though it sometimes appears that we live as exiles. Her "transparent humanness," a characteristic of her first-person narrative, allowed me to recognize that God is not just an observer, but rather an active participant in my own earthly pilgrimage.

The Great Divorce
by C. S. Lewis

In some Christian circles, it almost seems cliché that C. S. Lewis is recommended as much as he is–I find this rather to be a tribute to the writer who has done more for Christianity than any writer of the twentieth century. Personally, my sense of the credible possibility of heaven was fortified by *The Great Divorce.* To moderns, a place of reward and punishment after death seems archaic and superstitious; furthermore, a

God who judges souls and assigns them either to heaven or hell is an unpalatable and unfortunate invention of the ancients. Lewis offers a rarely considered perspective: the gates of hell are locked from the *inside*. In this brief narrative, the newly dead arrive at heaven's doorstep, where they are offered every opportunity to "taste and see that the Lord is good." Yet for reasons of reputation, vanity, resentment, and self-consciousness, among other things, they obstinately refuse paradise. The narrative reveals that its characters' destructive after-death choices are extensions of already established, life-long patterns. *The Great Divorce* challenges me to make my innumerable daily decisions well, for they will leave their mark "on that tiny central self which no one sees in this life but which each of us will have to endure—or enjoy—forever."

"Towards a Christian Aesthetic"
from *Unpopular Opinions*
by Dorothy Sayers

Sayers' "Towards a Christian Aesthetic" freed me from limiting assumptions I had unwittingly made about Jesus Christ. These assumptions were ones which I inherited, along with other beliefs, encouraged by a sort of childhood, Sunday-school acceptance that "God so loved the world. . . ." For many modern Christians, the narrative of the Great Passion seems saturated with a hierarchical image of Jesus, the Son, as somehow less than God, the Father—but not so for Sayers. In this piece, Sayers proves to be more succinct in her writing than she is in *The Mind of the Maker* (which also challenged my established beliefs in similar ways). She presents the possibility of an Incarnational view of the world, insisting that such an orientation is not original with her but resides at the very core of Scripture. Sayers' bold description of the implications of the Incarnation, ranging from nature to aesthetics, supports the notion that genuine Christians can and should be involved in such endeavors as philosophy, literature, education, and art. Sayer's work urges us to practice genuine Christian orthodoxy through understanding, first, what it really is.

Gene L. Green,
Biblical and Theological Studies

Poems and Prose of Gerard Manley Hopkins
by Gerard Manley Hopkins (Edited by W. H. Gardner)

When our undergraduate class was herded through Hopkins' poetry for the first time, my thoughts focused on reaching the luxuriant pastures of rest beyond the final exam. Hopkins' dense imagery frequently left me vexed from the strain of understanding. Convinced, however, that there was treasure to be found if I would only dig, I dug for years to come, at times using a thick dictionary as a pick. Bright, pure seams of gold were the prize. One of the most powerful English religious poets of the Victorian era, Hopkins offers verse that rumbles with the archetypal themes of creation, incarnation, and redemption, which bracket the corruption of the fall. This theologian cum poet pours upon the page the complex patterns of all that surrounds him, relying upon inspiration to lift him above common insight. In one of his most famous poems, "The Windhover," Hopkins envisions Christ: "I caught this morning morning's minion, king–/ dom of daylight's dauphin, dapple-dawn-drawn Falcon, in his riding." He circles in the high air, and then plunges down at the cross, only to shine forth with greater glory: "Brute beauty and valour and act, oh, air, pride, plume, here / Buckle! AND the fire that breaks from thee then, a billion / Times told lovelier, more dangerous, O my chevalier!"

The Jewish War
by Josephus
(G. A. Williamson, Translator; E. Mary Smallwood, Editor)

I think that reading books about other books can be wearisome. While secondary sources give neat summaries of the contents of great literature and carefully tell us the story of other times and places, there is nothing so refreshing as drinking from the wells of the primary sources. Why read books about the Bible before reading the Bible? And why read the multitude of tomes on the life and times of Jesus instead of reading the works of a first-century Jewish historian? In *The Jewish War*, Josephus puts us in touch with the violent times in which Jesus and the apostles ministered, introducing characters from the Idumean Herod the Great to the Roman Festus, and Jewish sects from the Sadducees to the Essenes. The labored and archaic translation of Josephus by Whiston is the most widely published. But give me the Williamson translation of *The Jewish War* for a good read about the events leading up to the first Jewish revolt, the sacking of cities from Gamla to Jerusalem under the leadership of Vespacian and Titus, and the fall of Masada in A.D. 73. Blood, mayhem, strife–all accounts become amazingly real, thanks to the ancient eyewitness and reporter.

A Theology of the New Testament
by George Eldon Ladd
(Edited by Donald A. Hagner)

Reading Ladd's *Theology* for the first time was like dragging a comb through my very disheveled theological hair. I had read the Bible often enough, but my theology was more traditional than biblical. Ladd set me straight on any number of issues, precisely because he took the pains to understand the writings of the New Testament on their own terms and turf. The original edition of *A Theology of the New Testament* was published in 1974, and the subsequent edition, edited by Hagner, does little more than bring the reader up to date on current discussions of the issues Ladd originally addressed. Hagner left the text itself alone– a good move. And save for his treatment of the Synoptic Gospels, Ladd's tome lacks any attempt to synthesize or compare the various New Testament authors on specific theological themes (as Donald Guthrie does in his comparable study). Useful essays by R. T. France on the theologies of "Matthew, Mark and Luke" and by David Wenham on "Unity and Diversity in the New Testament" address two issues unfortunately omitted from the original. All in all, this is a book of biblical theology, an attempt to let the New Testament writers speak without the imposition of some dogmatic formulation to make them say what they supposedly should.

Jeffrey K. Greenberg, Geology and Environmental Science

Habitation of Dragons
by Keith Miller

While not quite on a par with having to choose from among my five children, picking just a few good reads out of hundreds proves to be a challenging task. Tolkien's Trilogy and the precious novels of Chaim Potok should be read, of course. And so should Catherine Marshall's books. But my two winners deserve special acknowledgement, particularly by Christians. Instead of great fiction, my first selection falls into the category of a great devotional. *Habitation of Dragons*, by Keith Miller, has real power packed into a small number of pages. Miller was an "oil man" whose calling led him on to write and to speak about the work of Christ in our lives. This book emphasizes inner-life struggles or, as Miller calls them, "enemies." Our pride, feelings of guilt, mixed motives, loneliness, anxiety, fear, insecurity, and stubbornness are among the forty-two chapter themes. Each one begins with a brief story from Miller's experience—most are personal. The stories, serving as lessons, are followed by one or more pertinent quotations from famous individuals, a reflective prayer from Miller, and an incisive verse from Scripture. There are multitudes of good devotional books available, but none has been as inspirational for me as this one. Its lessons remain profound, and yet very realistic and practical, long after they are read. I have recently been pondering the significance of some of the book's stories. For example, the one I share most often with my students is about the sacrificial life of a small, plain woman. As a nurse, she made a humble career out of meeting the needs of mostly ill, elderly people. She is described as routinely providing enemas for invalids, opening her home for their care, and also challenging the generosity of a bishop to provide funds for her poor charges. Much like Mother Theresa, this woman's great humble spirit was the spark used by God to begin a powerful ministry. A similar theme is expressed in another story, this time of Miller's own failure in ministry and his loss of self-confidence. The lesson is revealed to the reader as Miller stands as a witness to Jesus, who takes over and redeems the situation. Miller and I share in some of the internal embarrassment and resentment that may come in serving others. For example, doing kind things can be often tedious, tiring, costly, and without earthly recompense. Although we may know that these feelings are part of the reality of ministry, we still harbor little nasty "dragons" inside. *Habitation of Dragons* touches many sore places. It makes you think, even when you believe you have arrived and are beyond learning from devotionals. The book will inspire the reader to consider keeping a journal on the inner life.

Annals of the Former World
by John McPhee

A great travelogue commentary, *Annals of the Former World* shines as a tour de force from author John McPhee. He has written something very impressive, here, and I am envious. The author of many books on the subject of earth science–my science–making it almost as exciting as the real thing, McPhee demonstrates his skill as a brilliant translator, not of language, but of an academic discipline. On a field trip, I could take you to see the beauty and genius of some aspect of Creation, but with less time and money to spend, you can experience the creation vicariously through the skillful prose of McPhee. This particular volume is a collection of five books, four previously available. Their essays, together in this volume, span the continental U.S. We travel along with the author as he learns from prominent geological experts. Stops are made at places of dramatic earth structure or regions with historical significance. The reader is treated to wonderful descriptions, with an artist's insight and appreciation. McPhee is so effective in communicating geology that, for my introductory geology course, I have considered scrapping the conventional textbook to replace it with *Annals*. As it is now, I refer to it and quote from it routinely for my students, particularly from the first two books, *Basin and Range* and *In Suspect Terrain*.

Em Griffin,
Communication

Man's Search for Meaning
by Viktor E. Frankl

When I came to Wheaton in 1970, most of my course load consisted of multiple sections of Public Address. I assigned a typical public speaking text, but I also made Frankl's short paperback required reading. I told students that it had little to do with giving speeches, but I was afraid they might graduate without having read the book. I later found out that it had as profound an impact on some of them as it did on me.

Viktor Frankl was an Austrian psychiatrist who, during World War II, was one of millions of Jews sent to a death camp. Yet through luck, fate, and divine providence–he credits all three–he repeatedly had what most captives did not, a chance to live. Frankl's book is both a grim and hopeful ethnography of life in Auschwitz–the interpreted experience of one who survived. The title of *Man's Search for Meaning* previews Frankl's conviction that "he who has a why to life can bear with almost any how." Frankl found that the vast majority of people who survived had a reason to live, be it a sense of mission from God, the burning hope of being reunited with a loved one, or even the chance for revenge against brutal captors. In Frankl's case *the will to meaning* came from a desire to publish what he was discovering about the human soul, findings that were only accessible to one who faces life and death decisions every day throughout years of privation. The first two-thirds of the book consists of narratives that could only be written by one who was there. Although describing dehumanizing captivity, the stories of camp life also reveal the humanizing choices that people can make when facing intolerable conditions and random brutality. Frankl refused to let his life be determined by the forces that constrained him. He insisted that no matter what the circumstances, we still have choice–even if it is only to choose our attitude toward God, fellow sufferers, or those who treat us as things. Coming from a man who experienced a living Hell, Frankl's message is one of hope rather than hatred. In the last third of the book, Frankl shifts from participant to observer. Based on his experience, he distills the psychological principles that define "logotherapy," his approach to counseling that centers on a client's need for meaning in life. He is convinced that healthy people are not driven by needs, but are drawn or pulled forward by their moral values. When in Poland last year, I made a decision to tour Auschwitz. Although some of my friends thought this excursion curious, I agree with Frederick Buechner's words: "Anyone who claims to believe in an all-powerful, all-loving God without taking into account this devastating evidence either that God is indifferent or powerless, or that there is no God at all, is playing games." My visit underlined the horror of existence without God. *Man's Search for Meaning* offers the possibility that small acts of love in the midst of our desperation are meaningful to God and to the people for whom he grieves.

Nancy A. Grisham, Christian Formation and Ministry

Life on the Highest Plane
by Ruth Paxson

A friend and mentor suggested this book to me when I was asking about the Holy Spirit and how to better communicate His role in our lives. As I began to read Paxson's writings, my heart was drawn closer and closer to Jesus. I realized this was much more than a book to help me articulate life in the Spirit–this would become a book God would use to help me know Him more intimately, understand His ways more clearly, and yield more fully to His Spirit within me. I have repeatedly returned to Paxson's themes on cleansing, yielding, faith, obedience, the Bible, and prayer, carefully considering their function in the process of helping me to be continually filled with the Holy Spirit. With great simplicity, this book lifts our eyes to the One who lives in us and longs for us to experience the fullness of His abundant life within us–*life on the highest plane.*

The Life You've Always Wanted
by John Ortberg

"God is not interested in your 'spiritual life.' God is just interested in your life." With these words, Ortberg provocatively captures God's intent for His completeness in every area of our lives. The book challenges the reader to pause, rest, and breathe a sigh of release . . . and relief. The result, for me, was the reminder that God loves me, and He is pleased. He longs for my doing to be energized by my being . . . in Him. However, some might question whether this approach promotes passivity. To the contrary, Ortberg is not writing about a passive life in Christ, but rather he points to a life of full engagement with God and others, a life transformed from the inside out by our relinquishment and cooperation with the One who loves us freely and fully. This book, too, truly lives up to its title: it has helped me experience *the life in Christ I've always wanted.*

Manya Gyuro,
Biblical and Theological Studies

Adiamante
by L. E. Modesitt, Jr.

As a teacher of Old Testament, I find exploring theology, principles, and ethics through biblical narrative one of the most exciting aspects of my work in the field. In a similar way, when I curl up in an easy chair with a modern American work of fiction, I am, more often than not, hoping to read a good story that makes me think. In Modesitt's *Adiamante*, I discovered a novel of depth that considers, through narrative, many of the issues humans face. Without going through odd convolutions to make his characters fit a particular ideal, Modesitt explores some of the compelling issues of our own time: the ecological system around us and the consequences of ignoring proper stewardship and care of the earth; the ethics and consequences of excess; the implications of virtual reality and cloning; the corrupting influence of power and how to counter it; and the responsibility of true leadership. Not all of the solutions presented in the novel may fit comfortably within an evangelical paradigm. Nevertheless, they prodded my own thinking with regard to how I choose to live as an individual, as a citizen, and as one who believes that God is the creator of the world and its inhabitants.

James Haltemann, Business and Economics

The Passions and the Interests
by Albert O. Hirschman

According to Albert Hirschman, to be civilized, society must find ways to successfully harness or repress the passions of humans. Before the modern era, philosophy and religion restrained the passions by cultivating virtue and a vision of life after death as reward for constructive social behavior. With modernity came skepticism that reason and religion could be the social glue. As human relationships became less personal, the notion that people pursue their own interests took center stage. Gradually, interests that were broadly defined evolved toward interests that were narrowly defined in terms of the acquisition of wealth. Finally, this pursuit of self-interest became the benevolent passion that subdued the less socially desirable passions. The liberal social structure featuring individual freedom and competition could now replace the old system of authority, obligation, and commitment. This new modern religion, liberal democratic capitalism, became the "savior" of the depraved passions of humanity. If the foregoing interpretation is correct, as Hirschman asserts, then it seems to me that Christians must ask several questions. Does Christianity add anything essential to the liberal systemic social glue? Are Christianity and liberal democratic capitalism competing or complementary explanations of how people should live? Does the "born again" experience alter the passions? These questions are ever present in all of my work.

The Worldly Philosophers
by Robert L. Heilbroner

Some books are informative, some profound. Some make the complex understandable, but only a few genuinely inspire. This classic book, first written in 1953, does all of the above, and it provided for me the encouragement to blend economics, history, and philosophy in my work. Heilbroner weaves his way through the history of economic thought from the Middle Ages through the 1970s by taking the reader into the streets of Europe and America. He skillfully connects the mundane to the broad strokes of philosophical analysis. The assumptions we make, the context from which we come, and the values we hold must be explored because they determine how we live. After reading this book, I felt as though I had expanded my understanding of the human provisioning process beyond the bounds of one discipline. In recent times I have had opportunity to spend some time with Professor Heilbroner, and though well past retirement age, he is still sharp and probing. After each conversation, no matter what the subject, I understood anew why Irving Howe regards "Robert Heilbroner as one of the two or three most perceptive, original, and lucid social analysts in America." *The Worldly Philosophers* is appropriate evidence for this claim.

The Life that Ruth Built
by Marshall Smelser

Occasionally someone comes along who can, almost single-handedly, alter institutions and how we think about those institutions. Babe Ruth altered baseball because he changed the game from a science to a game of passion. According to Smelser, in the period before Ruth, "People accepted success at managing a ball club as proof of superior knowledge of psychology and of the Science of Baseball. Science had become a religion, but its novices got it mixed up with engineering and called the teams machines." Babe Ruth altered that understanding of baseball forever. The fans loved Ruth, and he loved them back. This gave him an influence that baseball could not ignore. Ty Cobb's model of scratching out a low scoring victory with a single, stolen base, sacrifice bunt, and strategic baserunning lost its appeal when Babe Ruth made the home run the real thrill of the sport. The spontaneous excitement of the long ball brought more simple strategies and a reduced role for managers. Smelser presents the story of the boy from the Baltimore docks and the industrial boarding school playground with just the right balance of description and analysis. He meticulously tries to sort out fact from fiction while recognizing that both form the complex reality of the Babe. Immaturity, simple-mindedness, generosity and blind trusting are at once both positive and negative qualities, and in the end there are elements of betrayal and tragedy. This book forced me to examine anew the relationship of people and institutions, of spontaneity and life planning, and of character and circumstances.

Rolland Hein, English

Unspoken Sermons
by George MacDonald

All the writings of this Scottish master of mythopoetic works have done more for me in the shaping of my life than the writings of any other author. MacDonald is a master of mythopoeia, and all his writings view life anagogically. In his novels and fairy stories he presents a vision of Truth that arouses one's desire to live the life of a true person and defines the attitudes for doing so. I recommend them all, but if I must choose one title, I choose his sermons. They are not sermons in the traditional sense, but more like thoughtful personal essays in which one overhears the voice of one seeking for true understanding as he thinks his way through the central teachings of the Bible. His sermons summarize his vision and challenge the reader to quest for joy.

Mysticism
by Evelyn Underhill

In her thoroughly researched and knowledgeable survey of the Christian tradition of mysticism, Underhill delineates the soul of the Christian faith. It is not a creed, nor a rationally held set of opinions, but rather a deeply felt experience of the heart that is to be carefully tended and nurtured. She shows how the desire which God has placed in human hearts for Him has been pursued and developed by saintly people throughout the history of the Church. The mystical aspects of the Christian tradition are overlooked by many; this volume emphasizes their centrality. It is a Christian classic.

The Brothers Karamazov
by Fyodor Dostoyevsky

This novel is not a work of Christian propaganda, but rather a narrative that objectively presents the central issues and experiences of life, astutely showing, on the one hand, the responses to them of Christian faith, and, on the other, the main alternatives. It is primarily an expertly told story and must be read imaginatively and for pleasure, but Dostoyevsky's vision of the true nature of life is incisive and comprehensive. Its integrity arises from the felt reality of the characters and the true vision of human behavior. Through the narrative he explores such issues as the problem of human suffering, the purpose and value of freedom, and the nature of responsibility. Dostoyevsky's vision is probing and insightful. He is a Christian theologian in his own right.

P. J. Hill,
Business and Economics

A Conflict of Visions
by Thomas Sowell

How do we organize the facts we see in the world? What assumptions do we make about humans and human behavior? What theories of causation do we start with when we examine reality? Thomas Sowell, while writing as an economist, moves beyond the narrow issues that are usually the province of economics and discusses fundamental questions of worldview. He postulates that we operate with either a constrained or unconstrained vision of the world. Although there is much more to these categories than one might initially think, one fundamental difference is that the constrained person thinks in terms of tradeoffs and the unconstrained person more of solutions. I read this book in mid-career, after several decades of involvement in the economics profession. Sowell was extremely useful in helping me to understand my own thinking and that of other social scientists and policy makers. Although not writing as a Christian, he offers an analysis that fits well with the Christian belief that all people have certain theological assumptions by which they organize their thinking. I find myself continually referring back to his categories and his analysis when attempting to understand why people, when they discuss issues of power, equality, justice, and social process, can reach very different conclusions even though they analyze the same evidence.

Rich Christians in an Age of Hunger
by Ronald J. Sider

I initially encountered this book in its first edition, early on in my professional career as an economist. Sider's call to rich Christians to think carefully about their responsibilities to the poor of the world affected me deeply. I found myself continually under conviction as I read his call to biblical concern for those with less material resources. Although I did not always agree with Sider's economic analysis (which, I am pleased to note, has improved in subsequent editions), the heart of his message was clear and compelling, namely that we in the West are enormously rich compared to much of the world. Consequently, we have an obligation to share our wealth and to stand against unjust economic structures. Not only did Sider have an impact on my personal life, but my research career was also affected as I attempted to analyze and understand poverty and wealth around the world. This book is one that I have regularly referred to and used in my teaching.

Joshua P. Hochschild, Philosophy

Sex, Economy, Freedom & Community
by Wendell Berry

In a fragmented age, it is refreshing to be reminded of an underlying unity, and to be called to reintegrate our compartmentalized lives. Wendell Berry, the philosopher-farmer, does not want us to lose sight of the interpenetration of our biological, spiritual, economic, and social dimensions. That, anyway, is a way of summarizing in dispassionate academic terms the theme suggested by the more straightforward language of Berry's title: *Sex, Economy, Freedom & Community*. When I first read this collection, I was surprised at how effectively, and artfully, it changed the way I looked at the world and my own place in it. I have since read a good deal more of Berry, including his poetry and fiction, but I regularly return to the firm and gentle prose of his essays, and when I do it is with a combined sense of rejuvenation and guilt–as if I were consulting my own conscience. The peculiar force of Berry's prose is usually traced to his other roles, as farmer and poet; Berry's writing displays a poet's careful attention to words, and a sense of rootedness, humility, and care for creation. But together these do not explain the wisdom of a man who never loses sight of the whole. The immediate concerns of this collection range from the Gulf War, tobacco subsidies, and urban planning to sexual harassment, the theology of Genesis, and constitutional law. Ultimately, however, Berry is inviting us to reflect on the health of our bodies, our environment, our communities, and our souls–to reflect on where, and how, we live.

Edwin A. Hollatz, Communication

The Discoverers: A History of Man's Search to Know His World and Himself
by Daniel J. Boorstin

This highly provocative and encyclopedic volume brings together many episodes and issues over the history of mankind. The scope of this book is vast and its perspective magnificent. It is the kind of resource that any Christian student of the liberal arts should pick of and read. Of special significance to me is Part XIV, entitled "Opening the Past"; this section is comprised of several important chapters, including the following: "The Birth of History"; "Christianity Gives Direction"; and "Revising the Record." And Part XIII, "Widening the Communities of Knowledge," is also likely to be of great interest. And finally, "The Lost Arts of Memory" should engage anyone interested in the third branch of the liberal arts trivium–rhetoric. This is a captivating account of how human beings first discovered so many of the things that we take for granted today.

The Closing of the American Mind
by Allan Bloom

Many consider this to be a prophetic book. And while some of the indictments are subject to rigorous argument, nonetheless the author presents a reasoned and engaging critique of American higher education. This national best-seller asserts that the political and social crisis of the twentieth century is primarily one of the intellect. According to Bloom, higher education in America has lost its dedication to the humanities and has become increasingly fragmented. The Christian scholar should find Part II, "Nihilism, American Style," and especially the chapters on "Culture" and "Values," of particular interest. I found the final chapter, "The Student and the University," to be especially insightful and provocative. For anyone who wants to gain a better grasp of America's intellectual development within the ivy-covered walls of the university, particularly as it draws upon the Enlightenment, this book is a must read.

Strictly Speaking
by Edwin Newman

Christian scholars are first and foremost "workers with words." The key question is "How well do our words work for us?" Newman's trenchant critique of the use and misuse of language is most instructive and salutary. The problem is twofold, according to Newman, as represented by these important questions. First, do we fully recognize that our words have great consequences? And second, are we willing to change how we use words? Newman's answers to these questions are well worth the cost of the book. Newman's wit and wisdom, as always, will have a memorable impact upon the reader.

Arthur F. Holmes, Philosophy

Confessions
by St. Augustine

I first read the *Confessions* around 1950, and since then have come back to it again and again, always finding fresh insight on further dimensions of life and thought. At first blush it seemed a spiritual autobiography, a confession of sins and errors and an acknowledgement of God's goodness and wisdom, but then I learned it represents classical literature's first reflective narrative of the inner life. Initially, I read it as an essay on moral and religious psychology, but then I became caught up in scrutinizing my own inner motives and struggles. Again, at first I read it to get a handle on Augustine's theology, yet, soon I found myself chorusing his recurrent expressions of praise. As a reader, and one who has served the discipline of philosophy, I can identify and understand his reactions to the philosophies of his day, and how they pointed him toward an objective source for truth and morality. And I can see why Augustine says that faith is understanding's step, and understanding is faith's reward. Now, as I trace the reflections on his liberal learning and rhetorical training, Augustine makes me shun professional pride and selfish ambition. A line from the first paragraph puts it best: "You made us for yourself and our hearts find no peace until they rest in you."

The Idea of a University
by John Henry Newman

This is the classic that shaped my teaching career in the liberal arts, and for well over a century has stimulated thinking about the meaning and purposes of liberal education. Written for a new university that Newman had been asked to establish in Ireland, this apologia remains vitally relevant to problems in higher education today. Secularization resulting from Enlightenment rationalism had excluded theology from the curriculum in Newman's day, and a utilitarian view of learning questioned the value of knowledge without practical application for an industrial society. Not surprisingly, these issues are still with us, and Newman's arguments to the contrary are still persuasive. He rightly claims that theology is knowledge, too, and it is needed to understand and to complete the *universe* of learning, for which a *university* is named. If theology is neglected, then other disciplines will usurp its place—as indeed they already have. Liberal learning, moreover, is not only worthwhile for itself, argues Newman, but it also equips the mind with qualities like freedom, fairness, calmness, and wisdom. Thus, without teaching the particular skills of any one business, it helps fit one, as Milton wrote, in order "to perform all the offices, both private and public, of peace and war." (The more current editions of this book provide helpful and pertinent essays.)

Christ and Culture
by H. Richard Niebuhr

Is Christ, in whom I believe, for or against the culture in which I live? Must we always live with insurmountable tensions between Christ and culture? Or can not only people, but culture, too, be transformed? This book helped me—more than any other—in sorting out the alternatives and understanding the theology underlying my own and other people's views. For the historical account Niebuhr provides not only points up theological differences between Lutheran, Anabaptist, or Reformed perspectives, it also traces their roots to the New Testament, the early church, and, above all, the portrayed image of Christ himself. This is, in no usual sense, inspirational reading. Niebuhr's five types or ways of understanding Christ and culture are not as mutually exclusive as they first appear. Locating myself and my beliefs within the Grand Story, and its great cloud of witnesses, has given me an inspired sense of direction for living and working as a Christian in this troubled world.

Daniel Paul Horn,
Conservatory of Music

The Great Divorce
by C. S. Lewis

The written word, central though it may be to the development of knowledge and imagination, co-exists in my heart alongside stimuli affecting all the senses. Written words have indeed awakened me to the riches of the universe. Yet in that unfathomable part of me–known to God alone, which yearns to create because He has created–fragments of children's story, poetry, scripture, popular fiction, serious history, and stray song lyrics mingle with memories of that first experience of a Beethoven symphony, of swimming in the glowing colors of a Pacific sunset, and of the intoxicating aroma of Grandma's Moravian Christmas cookies. I am convinced that together they deeply inform who I am, and how I respond to the wonder all around me. Still, C. S. Lewis' slender volume of theological fiction comes to mind, a fantasy that presents Hell as a vast, gray town on the edges of darkness, populated by individuals who desire nothing more than isolation from each other. The denizens of Hell may take excursions to the outskirts of Heaven, and may choose to remain in the High Country itself. Through a series of conversations between spectral tourists and citizens of Heaven who they had known in life, Lewis proclaims a startling message: for most people, there is something they would rather keep at any cost rather than experience eternal joy on God's terms. As he reveals the secret motivations lurking behind the most banal of sins, Lewis inexorably draws the reader towards deep and honest self-examination. One scene, in particular, remains more vivid to me than virtually anything else in literature, telling me much about who I am as an artist, and about what I could become if left unchanged by Grace. Two artists encounter each other and begin a conversation. The visitor from Hell wishes to begin painting as soon as he arrives, but is told by his redeemed friend that he must wait until he learns once again to love the Reality around him more than his professional, aesthetic responses to it. "Every poet and musician and artist, but for Grace, is drawn away from the love of the thing he tells, to the love of the telling till, down in Deep Hell, they cannot be interested in God at all but only in what they say about Him." The discussion develops into an intellectual struggle for the ego, the ghostly artist finally choosing to continue a futile battle for fame and position in the darkness rather than accepting obscurity along with everlasting love and light in God's presence. I have yet to find a more succinct or insightful description of the particular snares of the artistic life. Though I have been a Christian and an artist for many years now, I still stumble and find myself struggling for professional position and status, forgetting that I am already in Christ, the only position that ultimately matters. I still need this book to remind me of the insidious power of artistic temptations.

Paul R. House,
Biblical and Theological Studies

New Testament Introduction
by Donald Guthrie

Books influence us for different reasons at different times of our lives. When I was a college student, I was already preaching and serving in churches. I was also majoring in biblical studies at a wonderful college that did not always stress academic approaches to the Scriptures. Indeed, at times our teachers treated scholarship as a necessary evil, though they instilled in us a love for the Bible and for people. Thus, when I was assigned Guthrie's book in a Pauline Literature course, I entered a new and interesting world. Guthrie wrestles vigorously with such major scholarly issues as the authorship, date, and theology of the books of the New Testament. Thus, Guthrie gave me knowledge of scholarly works and ideas. He also convinced me that conservative scholarship deserves consideration and admiration. While doing so he offered me a model of careful, fair, thorough, generous writing, full of conviction, and he proved that there is no reason to divorce serious scholarship from service in the church. In short, the book helped start me on the path to an academic career, something I could not have known at the time. It also helped me stay connected to the local church. Though Guthrie's book is now a bit dated, it continues to inspire me to rise to its standard of excellence. Few similar works equal its breadth of knowledge, and the day may be gone when individual authors attempt such a project.

14609-DAVI

God, Revelation and Authority: Volume Five, God Who Stands and Stays
by Carl Henry

Once we start our careers and have some success in them, we often take strategic turns in what we emphasize. After several years of teaching at Taylor University, I was asked to write a volume on Old Testament theology, so I thought that I should read more widely in theological fields than I had done previously. One of the authors I explored was Carl F. H. Henry, who has written or edited over forty volumes. All Henry's books display a concern for stating foundational principles, employing impeccable logic, composing telling prose, and challenging readers with the implications of their beliefs. Above all, however, Henry makes God the primary topic of his books. And *God, Revelation and Authority* may be his clearest and richest expression of God's character, authority, and goodness. Henry establishes his belief that God is real and that human beings can speak coherently and accurately about God. How? By adhering to the Scriptures. Perhaps his best chapter is the third, "The Living God of the Bible," which expounds upon the very title. Everything else he writes, whether about God's attributes or nature, flows from this biblical portrait. For Henry, if evangelical theology does not depict the one living God as the Scriptures describe him, then the movement has been a waste of time. When I first read Henry I knew what I wanted my own writing to do: make God known.

The Memory of Old Jack
by Wendell Berry

No one can predict exactly what life will bring. But we can expect difficulties of some sort, or even outright suffering. During such a time in my life I returned to the reading of literature, a habit I had largely left behind after graduate school to pursue theological studies. At that time I sought perspective on the whole of life, as found in perceptive writers.

I had read three or four of Wendell Berry's books before I discovered Old Jack. The story is told from the perspective of a ninety-two-year-old farmer reflecting on his life. In his time Jack was a farmer, husband, father, lover, and valued community member. He suffered for his own mistakes and for the mistakes of others. Coming from a rural background myself, I identified with Berry's multifaceted treatment of country life. I was drawn to Jack's personal sense of achievement and failure, of gains and losses, of isolation and community. Jack survived, and he also passed on wisdom. When death comes he is neither alone nor dependent. This book helped me realize that a few years of very hard times do not make a life. Rather, it is the people, the community, the beliefs, and the character we derive from life that matters then. Old Jack did not know such things naturally; he had to learn them. As I read how he learned them, I learned them too.

Bruce Howard,
Business and Economics

Selected Works
by George Herbert Morrison

George Herbert Morrison is without question the most influential author in my life. A prominent Scottish pastor who lived from 1866 to 1928, he honed his command of the English language when, as a young man, he assisted Sir James Murray in the creation of *The Oxford English Dictionary* (better known as the *OED*). How can I describe his work? Writing with incredible precision, he addresses theological issues with enough substance and depth to keep you thinking for days after you put one of his books down. In fact, I have found that I simply cannot mine all that is there on the initial reading. (This may be why I have read some of his books three times!) And as I read, I am struck with the wonderful sense of pragmatism that is conveyed through his poetic prose, which trickles down like water from the Scottish highlands. I especially recommend *Highways to Heaven*, *Wings of Glory*, *Floodtides*, *Meditations on the Gospels*, *More Meditations on the Gospels*, or *Sunday Evenings in the City Pulpit*. Whether you have fifteen minutes or fifteen hours, I believe you will greatly profit from an investment of time in any one of Morrison's books.

Alan Jacobs, English

Black Lamb and Grey Falcon: A Journey through Yugoslavia
by Rebecca West

In the late 1930s, Rebecca West made several visits to Yugoslavia, ultimately covering every province of the country, keeping a journal along the way. She envisioned a "short book" on the country, but ended up writing one of the largest, most ambitious, and greatest books of the twentieth century. In *Black Lamb and Grey Falcon*, West would combine her journeys into one, changing names, linking events, amplifying characters but also spinning marvelous cadenzas about key moments in the history of the South Slavs. Especially powerful is her account of the catastrophic defeat of the Serbs by the Ottoman Turks on the plain of Kossovo in 1389. (In the Vrdnik monastery in the Frushka Gora of Serbia, West saw, still lying in state, the headless body of Prince Lazar, who led the Serbs in that debacle. She touched his blackened and desiccated hand.) West's story is the encounter of the liberal mind with something much older, something ultimately alien to it. As she goes deeper into Serbia—a culture that she loves passionately—she sees more and more clearly a side of this culture that remains dark and inexplicable to her. She thinks, above all, of the strange fact that Prince Lazar is the greatest hero in Serbian history, not in spite of but because he lost the battle: as West presents it, the prophet Elijah, in the form of a grey falcon, demands that Lazar choose between an earthly and a heavenly kingdom, and he chooses the latter. To the Serbs this is an act of great courage and piety, since the blood of so many of Lazar's people will therefore be on his hands; but West reflects that "If this disposition to be at once Christ and Judas is inborn . . . we might as well die, and the sooner the better, for the defeat is painful after the lovely promise." A few years earlier, West had written an angry and sometimes scornful biography of St. Augustine; but here, she comes very close to an Augustinian view of the fallen world. She does not, I believe, understand all that she sees; but she sees with a clarity almost unparalleled in this century. When she finished her manuscript in early 1941, it was almost half-a-million words long. This was unfortunate, because in the midst of the war paper was being strictly rationed. But West's publishers, Macmillan of London, seem not to have hesitated: they were utterly compelled by the narrative. As her editor wrote, "Who would not be [compelled] by a book which demonstrated by its argument that the East End of London would not be lying in ruins if the Balkan Christian powers had not been defeated by the Turks in 1389?"

The Gospel in a Pluralist Society
by Lesslie Newbigin

In his biography of Newbigin, Geoffey Wainwright explains, "As rarely in modern times, the Church had in Lesslie Newbigin a bishop-theologian whose career was primarily shaped by his evangelistic and pastoral responsibilities and who yet made contributions to Christian thought that match in interest and importance those of the more academic among his fellow bishops and teachers. Their origin and destination in practice is what gave and continues to give such an extraordinary resonance to the oral and literary products of Newbigin's creative mind and loving heart." Having served for almost forty years as a pastor and then bishop in the Church of South India, Newbigin had an intimate daily acquaintance with a thoroughly pluralistic society; so when, after his "retirement" and return to his home country of England, he began a second career as a prolific writer on theology and missions, he had a great fund of Christian pastoral experience on which to draw. Because Newbigin tried always in his writing to be faithful to that practical context of Christian witness and teaching, his work on pluralism and "postmodernity"–a term for which he seems to have had little use–has a depth and richness missing from most theological treatments of the subject. He draws heavily on the work of such thinkers as Alasdair MacIntyre and Michael Polanyi, but always places them in the context of the universal Christian vocation to mission and evangelism. All of his books are valuable, but *The Gospel in a Pluralist Society* is the most sweeping and incisive. One of its chapter titles sums up what I love about Newbigin's work: "The Congregation as Hermeneutic of the Gospel." For Newbigin, the interpretation of Scripture is not something done primarily through the writing of commentaries or theological treatises; rather, it is the work of the ordinary congregation of believers who show what their interpretation of Scripture is by their everyday words and deeds. The unique value of Newbigin's work lies in its connection between sophisticated intellectual reflection and those "everyday words and deeds."

Lee D. Joiner,
Conservatory of Music

The Healing Presence:
How God's Grace Can Work in You to Bring
Healing in Your Broken Places
and the Joy of Living in His Love
by Leanne Payne

It is a paradox that a book about "Incarnational Reality" starts with a chapter entitled "Celebrating Our Smallness." Feeling depleted from the academic year and aware of my need for renewal, I began a summer reading of Payne's book and found myself drawn into a compelling argument for revitalizing the practice of the presence of God. She observes that modern Christians at times fall into the "disease of introspection," which leads to a conundrum: we "practice the presence of ourselves." This book is a tapestry woven with Scripture as a foundation, scholarly and literary quotations, and case studies that reveal the grace of God at work in the lives of individuals. Payne draws on a wealth of knowledge of literature, especially the fiction and nonfiction of C. S. Lewis, and the unique insights gained through her close relationship with Clyde Kilby, the now legendary chair of the English Department at Wheaton College. There is much in this book that feeds the rational mind, yet there is the recognition that symbols and imagery are agents for conveying God's grace to us. "Reality is simply far too great to be contained in propositions," writes Payne. As a musician whose challenge is to balance technique and analysis with expression and gestures in sound, I delighted in this affirmation of our multi-faceted relationship to God.

Restoring the Christian Soul: Overcoming Barriers to Completion in Christ through Healing Prayer
by Leanne Payne

My reading of Leanne Payne's companion volume, *Restoring the Christian Soul,* was a transforming encounter with the cross of Christ. Building upon the foundation laid in the earlier book, it delves into barriers that limit our growth toward spiritual maturity, including the failure to accept oneself and the inability to extend or receive forgiveness. This book is not an easy read, as it takes you down into the trenches where the battles rage. Examples illustrating her points are detailed and intense. She chronicles how self-acceptance, the first step in the journey, was taught "as a virtue to be attained"; its opposite, self-hatred, is but "a substitute for humility." The terrain she covers is not new, but she succeeds in focusing the issues squarely around theological truths. I was forced to ascertain whether the doctrine I understood had penetrated my heart when I read, "Our hearts need to picture these great and grave actions (the crucifixion and resurrection) of Christ aright, for they image the great story of our salvation." I came away from this book with the sense that the healing God desires to bring to our lives is fuller than I had ever imagined—completing all areas of life, even our imagination.

Keith Jones, English

Winesburg, Ohio
by Sherwood Anderson

Whenever I read *Winesburg, Ohio*, I become convinced that Sherwood Anderson must have intently studied the work of William Faulkner, Flannery O'Connor, and Wendell Berry. Then I recall that the work was published in 1919, six years before O'Connor was born, ten years before *The Sound and the Fury* was published, and fifteen years before the birth of Berry. The work is profoundly modern, and its influence is evident in these (and other) authors. In this collection of short stories, Anderson seemingly effortlessly weaves together the lives of Winesburg's inhabitants into a unified whole. Each of the characters is, in the term the work uses, a grotesque: a human being who has attempted to make one part of the world be the whole world. Anderson uses George Willard, who interacts with most of the other people in the work, to show the paradox of isolated individuals living in a community—an idea which is reflected in the form of *Winesburg, Ohio* itself—isolated short stories forming a work larger than the sum of its parts. When I first taught the book, this idea fired my imagination because I saw it reflected not only in the class I was teaching, but in the entity of any institution of higher education—not, I should note, because I saw my students, myself, or other members of the faculty and staff as grotesques. Rather, I saw what individuals surrender and what they gain by putting themselves into any community. The characters in the book are intensely likable and down to earth, but their outward simplicity belies the complexity of each, and the even greater complexity of the relationships between them.

Ex Libris:
Confessions of a Common Reader
by Anne Fadiman

The eighteen essays in this volume articulate, in a humorous but not insignificant way, the relationship between books and their owners. The first essay, "Marrying Libraries," details how, after six years of marriage, the separate libraries the author and her husband had kept on opposite sides of their New York City loft merged into one. For the most part, Anne and George were able to agree on how the marriage of the books was to take place. "We ran into trouble, however, when I announced my plan to arrange English literature chronologically but American literature alphabetically by author." Fadiman's desire to see the development of English literature through the centuries–reflected in the shelves she encountered every day–is one I can readily appreciate, just as my wife can appreciate George's desire to find a book by a given author without first having to know when the work was written. The topics of the other essays range from how the way we treat books reveals something about us (her own copy of *The Joy of Cooking* contains "part of the *actual egg yolk* that my daughter glopped into her very first batch of blueberry muffins"), to why we desire to read books in the books' settings (I am envious of her friend who read Book Nine of *The Odyssey* in the cave considered to be the Cyclops'), to how children acquire their taste for reading. Fadiman's work inspires me to read more and to think more about what I'm reading. If the number of other good books recommended in this work seems overwhelming, then read Fadiman first–she will inspire you to read all the others.

Ken Kalisch,
Christian Formation and Ministry

Man's Search For Meaning
by Viktor E. Frankl

Some have read this book during college, as it has long been a popular text. Still, it is worth reading again after college, sure to challenge the reader with truth essential to maintaining a life worth living. *Man's Search For Meaning* is written in two parts. First, Dr. Frankl provides a thoughtful account of three long years as a prisoner in a Nazi concentration camp. This is followed by an introduction to the theory of "logotherapy" which Frankl developed as a result of his camp experience. The book is essential reading because it searches the very waters of our spiritual life, from the weedy shallows to the ocean depths. It is the testimony of a man who has suffered greatly, yet who has turned that suffering into service. Frankl is an excellent model for us all. He reminds us that life is not fair or easy, but difficult: "Suffering is an ineradicable part of life." But out of the trials of life can come meaning and direction. He offers us hope in the midst of tribulation. He prods us to take responsibility for our lives, remembering that we always have a choice of action: "Everything can be taken from a man but one thing: the last of the human freedoms—to choose one's attitude in any given set of circumstances, to choose one's own way . . . It is such an externally difficult situation which gives man the opportunity to grow spiritually beyond himself." Such words will surely be an encouragement to those who seek to thrive rather than merely survive.

In the Name of Jesus
by Henri J. M. Nouwen

Destined to become a Christian classic, this book on leadership was written only a few years ago. It is short, easy to read, and utterly convicting–good medicine for the soul of those seeking to live wholeheartedly for "Christ and His Kingdom." Henri Nouwen was a scholar and priest at Harvard University for many years until he asked himself this question: Does becoming older bring me closer to Jesus? His answer was no. So he moved from Harvard to a L'Arche community for the mentally handicapped– "from the best and the brightest, wanting to rule the world, to live with men and women who had few or no words and were considered, at best, marginal to the needs of our society." Here he was given "new words to use in speaking about Christian leadership in the future." Nouwen's words to us are ones of profound wisdom, certainly at odds with current culture. He challenges us "to move from a concern for relevance to a life of prayer, from worries about popularity to communal and mutual ministry, and from a leadership built on power to a leadership in which we critically discern where God is leading us and our people." It is the image of "a vulnerable leader" and "a trusting leader. . . . the leader with outstretched hands, who chooses a life of downward mobility." Revisit this book frequently, as I do, to be reminded of leadership style that is truly out of this world!

Kathleen Kastner, Conservatory of Music

The Art of Forgiving: When You Need to Forgive and Don't Know How
by Lewis B. Smedes

Someone recommended this book to me, and when I read it, I realized that it really answers so many questions that we have about *what* forgiveness is and *how* to experience it. Smedes asks the questions, "What are we actually doing when we forgive someone? What does that mean? And what doesn't it mean?" He looks at the kinds of actions we forgive and most importantly, he emphasizes and explains the importance and process of forgiveness. As he notes, one can't all of a sudden say, "I forgive you." In fact, this book takes the reader through the process, making it easier to understand what you *are* doing and what you *are not* doing when you forgive another. You are going through the stages of surrender, but you are not necessarily forgetting what the other person has done. Smedes points out that sometimes we say that we are forgiving, when in fact there is nothing really to forgive. Realizing that there are some offenses that I need to forgive and other circumstances that I really don't need to worry about was particularly helpful to me. Additionally, some people are afraid of forgiving because they think it means, "Well, I have to get back in touch with this person and we have to make things right to the extent that we are friends again." But Smedes says this is not the case: to forgive an offense does not mean I have to get back into a relationship with the offender. One of the helpful aspects of this book is that the author uses a variety of beneficial illustrations–from describing horrendous circumstances that people have gone through to minor kinds of things. Regardless of the offense, Smedes convincingly points out that if I don't forgive another, ultimately, I am the one who suffers for it; the importance of forgiving is really not for the other person, but for me, precisely because it frees me up. And once free, I can move on with my life. Smedes makes the interesting point that forgiveness can be administered without the offender knowing. For example, if you have a parent or loved one who has passed away, you can forgive that person without that person being around to help you through the process. Finally, Smedes has an important section on forgiving ourselves–this is so crucial because we can take a long time to forgive ourselves for things we've done that keep us from experiencing freedom in our lives. I read this book at a time when I was going through some struggles with the church. And, as Smedes points out, you can't forgive institutions; you forgive people. This book came to me at a perfect time when I had the opportunity to apply its principles directly to my life. Since that time, I have been able to recommend this book to several friends who, like me, have been hurt and have needed to know the power of true forgiveness.

Tom Kay,
History

Christianity and Classical Culture: A Study of Thought and Action from Augustus to Augustine
by Charles Norris Cochrane

I usually identify this book as most important to me in the development of my ideas regarding the significance of Christianity, historically, in contemporary culture and personally. I first came across it as an undergraduate student, but it was as a graduate student and a beginning teacher that I truly read it in its entirety. Woven together are the presentations of philosophies of the ancient world, classical perspectives on historical writing, the search for meaning in political action, and the truly revolutionary impact of Christianity–"a new thing." Cochrane shows that "the discovery of personality was, at the same time, the discovery of history. For by giving significance to individual experience, it gave significance also to the experience of the race, thereby providing a clue to the meaning and direction of the historical process. To the Christians, however, this clue was to be found, not in any figment of the human mind, but in the revelation of Christ, accepted as . . . the true *logos* or account of being and movement in the universe." By rereading this book and discovering something new on each occasion, I continue to be influenced and sharpened by Cochrane's writing; like no other author, he has helped me understand the significance of the impact of Christianity upon the ancient world, and upon the ideas and actions of subsequent ages.

Main Currents in Modern Political Thought
by John H. Hallowell

Long before it became fashionable to state forthrightly one's religious convictions in academic publications, Professor Hallowell did so in 1950. Unique to this textbook is his Christian critique of the basic ideas of frequently cited primary sources and the several interpretations other scholars have given them. In the concluding section, the author not only describes the plight of mid-twentieth century political realities as a moral issue, "The Crisis of Our Times," but he also identifies a variety of Christian responses that might serve as a basis for a truly Christian social order. Anglicanism (his own personal preference) is clearly set apart from Roman Catholicism and several Protestant alternatives as a theological basis for Christian society. Hallowell's work has been a significant stimulus not only to my academic life, but also to my civic participation and my ongoing critique of contemporary Christian social and political perspectives. As Professor Hallowell puts it, "The sinfulness of man should not be used as a cloak for indifference nor as an excuse for lack of thought, of effort or of courage."

Sharon Kim,
English

The Sickness Unto Death
by Soren Kierkegaard

While doing my laundry one day, I opened *The Sickness Unto Death* and read it in what seemed a single flash. Kierkegaard showed me two things. First, that it is possible to be a Christian and a brilliant philosopher at the same time. I had long been skeptical about worldly wisdom, especially in the form of Christian philosophy, but this book changed my mind. Second, he answered a question that had been in my heart: How is it that, as a Christian who knows and passionately believes the promises of God, I could still be prone to despair? I don't mean depression; I mean existential despair. Doesn't the Lord provide ultimate meaning, not to mention love, joy, and peace? With quiet eloquence, Kierkegaard writes of "despair, this sickness of the self, this sickness unto death." He writes in philosophical terms, dialectically considering, for example, a "gradation in the consciousness of the self" or describing "pure immediacy or immediacy containing a quantitative reflection." Yet what emerges is a clear, thoroughly-considered, finely-felt understanding of a central, defining aspect of Christianity, "that the opposite of sin is not virtue but faith." This book deepened my understanding of the gospel, leaving me refreshed, edified, and changed.

The Iliad and *The Odyssey*
by Homer
(Translated by Robert Fitzgerald)

As a freshman in college, I disdained the classics of the Western tradition and thus didn't read them. I preferred more modern and decadent fare, like Oscar Wilde. But years later I looked into Fitzgerald's Homer and understood for the first time that there really is such a thing as Literature (with a capital L) and that there is indeed a blend of truth, beauty, and goodness so sublime as to become Art. Like two halves of a globe, *The Iliad* and *The Odyssey* offer a vision of life–one in a time of war (*Iliad*) and one in a time of peace (*Odyssey*), working out the boundaries of what an ideal individual should be in each. Both epics elegantly juxtapose the smallest number of elements to produce the most complete and complex understanding of earthly existence–physical, emotional, intellectual, moral, social, political, personal, familial, cultural, geographical, historical, aesthetic, and religious. Yet the marvel of these epics is not that they include many different aspects of life, but that they are able to relate these life elements in a wise and beautiful proportion. For perspective and artistry, Homer's epics are simply the best.

Cynthia Neal Kimball, Psychology

Hinds' Feet On High Places
by Hannah Hurnard

As I was journeying through a painful period in my life, my son offered me his copy of *Hinds' Feet on High Places*. This book is a wonderful allegory, written many years ago. It is a story of Much-Afraid as she takes God's word seriously in Habakkuk 3:19: "I will make thy feet like hinds' feet and set thee upon thine High Places." Much-Afraid is crippled and frightened about most everything in her life. She doesn't know how to follow this Great Shepherd who asks so much. She will undergo a journey to receive hinds' feet, which will allow her to prance with the Shepherd on High Places. To help her, he provides two companions, one named Sorrow and the other Suffering. I imagine Much-Afraid taking their hands timidly as she begins her journey through many wildernesses. The narrator says, "How could one follow a person who asked so much, who demanded such impossible things who took away everything. If she went down there, as far as getting to the High Places was concerned, she must lose everything she had gained on the journey so far." And when the journey takes a turn for the worse (or so it seems), she is asked, "Will you bear this too, Much-Afraid? Will you suffer yourself to lose or to be deprived of all that you have gained on this journey to the High Places? Will you go down this path of forgiveness into the Valley of Loss, just because it is the way that I have chosen for you? Will you still trust and still love me?" She knows that she will not go back. Although she is no longer sure how the Great Shepherd will complete his promise to her, she chooses to continue to trust him: "Strangely enough, down there in the Valley of Loss, Much-Afraid felt more rested, more peaceful, and more content than anywhere else on the journey. It seemed, too, that her two companions also underwent a strange transformation. They still held her hands, but there was neither suffering nor sorrow in their touch."

The Return of the Prodigal Son: A Story of Homecoming
by Henri J. M. Nouwen

After a challenging time of struggle with mental, emotional, and spiritual pain, Henri Nouwen penned this profoundly moving meditation. Using Rembrandt's remarkable painting of the prodigal son, Nouwen writes of homecoming, affirmation, and reconciliation. What struck me most was the idea of learning to give love as the father gave love while also learning to receive love as the prodigal received love. In my more honestly reflective moments, I realize that I still want the Father to take care of me, just as the father in the story took care of the prodigal. I can relate so much more to the prodigal as a character, fully repentant, bargaining to compensate for his sin. But God calls us to become that prodigal's father, at times, too, loving others fully and without conditions of worthiness. Nouwen warns us that this position–of the caring father– can also be a lonely one. From experience, I think he is right. And yet, if I'm to grow spiritually, I must allow God to shape me and make me more like the character of the father. Henri Nouwen takes a rich parable of love and forgiveness and transforms it into an inspirational meditation on spiritual growth and personal development.

Carol Kraft, Foreign Languages

Momo
by Michael Ende

Sent to me from Munich by a former student, this work was almost immediately added to my reading list for the twentieth century. Its vivid, lively portrayal of our ever increasing, frenzied life-style is countered by Momo, the youthful, never anxious, character with the healing presence. This young but wise listener senses that something is amiss in the world of adults. The author paints colorful images of adults caught in the lie that time can be saved for later. In this work we see such adults change from human beings into robot-like figures, caught in a vicious cycle, incapable of change. However, like many fairy tales, this one has a happy ending, much to the reader's joy and relief. The story challenges us to reflect on our own context, and to seriously consider the wisdom of the phrase, "the slower, the faster." Ultimately, *Momo* brings us face to face with a life that has been robbed of what is vital for human fulfillment, prompting us not to make an idol of time.

David E. Lauber,
Biblical and Theological Studies

Lest Innocent Blood be Shed: The Story of the Village of Le Chambon and How Goodness Happened There
by Philip Hallie

This is a beautiful book. It recounts the remarkable story of a small, remote, and seemingly insignificant town in southern France. In contrast to the dark and terrible violence of World War II, the villagers of Le Chambon, under the guidance of pastor André Trocmé, peacefully and unassumingly saved thousands of Jewish children and adults from certain death. The action of these villagers represents nothing other than a miracle of God's grace. There is nothing naïve nor sentimental about this portrayal of this simple yet heroic response to persons in great need. Perhaps the most significant impression this story has made on me is the manner in which the residents of Le Chambon carried out their task with singleness of heart, and in a way that did not draw attention to themselves. Further, their actions were not intended to demonstrate or enhance their own goodness nor contribute to their personal righteousness; here we see genuine humility. The efforts of the villagers embody a faithful and grateful response to the gospel and a deep love for Jesus. Trocmé and the townspeople were committed to the well-being of the Jews and to nonviolence because they desired "not to be separated from Jesus." This intimacy with Jesus is profoundly seen in Hallie's observation, "Jesus was for Trocmé the embodied forgiveness of sins, and staying close to Jesus meant always being ready to forgive your enemies instead of torturing and killing them."

Evangelical Theology:
An Introduction
by Karl Barth

This slim volume offers the wise and mature insights of arguably the most significant theologian of the twentieth century, Karl Barth. It states in clear and simple language how we ought to approach the theological task. Barth's description of "evangelical" theology demonstrates an unwavering commitment to speaking about Immanuel–God with us. The God who encounters us and reveals himself to us in the gospel, as attested in the New Testament, is, as Barth insists, the proper object of theological reflection. Although one might not, and perhaps ought not, agree fully with every detail of Barth's immense *Church Dogmatics*, this precis of his theological project will serve as a powerful and positive reminder that theology essentially is a response to God's turning toward us and speaking to us. Theology indeed involves rigorous study, faithful explication of Holy Scripture, and service to God's Word, the Church, and the world; however, from beginning to end, Barth tells us, theology is an act of prayer. This collection of lectures and essays will not only benefit academic theologians; it will also enrich every thoughtful Christian who acknowledges that all attempts to understand God, his truth, and his grace, must take place on one's knees.

Steven L. Layne, English

Molder of Dreams
by Guy Rice Doud

Never have I read a more thought-provoking treatise on the power we have to make an impact on another, for better or worse, than in this stirring autobiography by Guy Rice Doud. This 1986 National Teacher of the Year shares much more than classroom vignettes. He takes his readers on a personal trek that begins in a volatile home, ignited by the fear and devastation of alcoholism, then moves forward through tragedy and triumph. The poignant ending is certain to leave an indelible impression on anyone who has ever stood at the front of a classroom. In speaking of this book, I often say that after every chapter I am either weeping or laughing–and it is true. Doud's tales, highlighting his colorful small-town roots, are charming, and the spiritual guidance and wisdom offered by his grandparents will resonate with any discerning reader. I classify this work as a "must-read" for teachers at every level, preschool to graduate school. I recommend it, as well, to any readers who are willing to consider just how great an opportunity Christ has given teachers to touch the lives of those around them. This is one book to read again and again.

Jillian N. Lederhouse, Education

The Dialectic of Freedom
by Maxine Greene

One of the most influential books I have read in the past ten years has been Maxine Greene's *The Dialectic of Freedom*, which has had a profound impact on my view of education in a democracy. Greene defines human freedom as the capacity to surpass the given and look at things as if they could be otherwise. In contrast to liberty, which Greene sees as more individualistic, freedom involves choices and actions that are grounded in community. Citizens in a free society are able to envision a better world and work to achieve it. Quite the opposite, oppression exists when certain citizens are prevented from setting life goals and accomplishing them. Through the poetry of Langston Hughes and others, Greene paints a portrait of the African American experience that depicts the struggle to realize the vision of another life. Similarly, through the works of Emily Dickinson and others, Greene sketches a picture of women's efforts to create the space in their busy, detail-filled lives in order to dream of a different existence. From these portraits, Greene invites educators to challenge the routine practices of schooling in order to construct a learning community where all students are free to dream and free to achieve their goals. After reading this book and reflecting on Greene's conceptualization of freedom, I realized more fully the significant work that teachers are called to do each day in classrooms across our nation.

Kathryn Long, History

Essays of E. B. White
by E. B. White

I picked up the *Essays of E. B. White* while I was working on my Ph.D., at a time when I felt overwhelmed by the jargon of academia and was afraid I might get swallowed up in it. White's *Essays*, a collection of pieces mostly from *The New Yorker*, provided a necessary antidote. They were not scholarly reflections. White was an unpretentious observer of ordinary American life during the first two-thirds of the twentieth century, and some of his best writing recounts adventures on his Maine farm. The author of *Charlotte's Web* knew about animals and barnyards and boats. He also had a nearly perfect ear for the English language. In "Bedfellows," about a morning spent sick at home, White writes, "on occasions like this I am almost certain to be visited by the ghost of Fred, my dash-hound everlasting, dead these many years. In life, Fred always attended the sick, climbing right into bed with the patient like some lecherous old physician, and making a bad situation worse." Not only Fred, but also ghosts of raccoons, elderly gray geese, New England railroads, and Walden Pond haunt these essays. White's *Essays* and other collections of his writing became a part of my recreational reading throughout graduate school. They kept me grounded. Every once in a while, I still reach for White's essays in order to remember the plain beauty of a well-crafted sentence.

Uncle Tom's Cabin
by Harriet Beecher Stowe

I didn't intend to become fascinated by *Uncle Tom's Cabin.* I hated the caricatured version of the story in the filmed musical "The King and I," and I knew that, for all her skills as a writer and passionate opposition to slavery, Harriet Beecher Stowe still shared many of the prejudices of her day. Then I read the book and was stunned by Stowe's theological astuteness and the power of her characters. Her picture of God combined vivid images of wrath and mercy. The thundering of the Old Testament prophets existed alongside God-the-nurturing-parent, as represented by the Quaker mother Rachel Halliday, who gently cared for the weak and oppressed. Stowe accomplished an amazing feat by making Uncle Tom the first black Christ figure in American literature. Cheap theater and vaudeville acts later diminished Uncle Tom as a symbol, but Stowe's original was a man of dignity and strength. "Didn't I pay down twelve hundred dollars cash, for all there is inside yer old cussed black shell? An't yer mine, now, body and soul?," asks Simon Legree. Tom's reply is clear: "No! no! no! my soul an't yours, Mas'r!" Tom's soul belonged to God alone. The book pushed me to explore the true nature of Christian submission, and it reinforced my commitment to understanding the contributions of women like Stowe to American history.

David Maas, History

Selected Works
by Bruce Catton

My personal encounter with Clio, the female muse of history, began around the sixth grade when our family began to visit historical sites. It was after tramping around the Gettysburg Battlefield that I fell in love with history. By junior high, I eagerly read all of Bruce Catton's books on the Civil War, titles such as *The Coming Fury, Terrible Swift Sword* and *A Stillness at Appomattox*. At the time I probably did not fully comprehend how much these books shaped my life. My high school history courses were boring. Fortunately, they are a blur in my collective memory. I recall courses full of facts (names and dates) but never tales of flesh-and-blood people struggling with real dreams, goals, frustrations, and victories. Catton discovered that history was about stories, using the narrative style. When I started teaching in 1970 at Wheaton College, I kept reminding myself that teaching history involves storytelling. I have found that students remember a tale that is rich in details better than just a skeletal list of the causes of the Civil War. Illustrating each point in a lecture outline with true-life stories makes history come alive. Since most stories portray humanity in a sinful, fallen world and, at the same time, how grace and courage allow people to triumph, often a Christian history teacher can naturally integrate biblical principles into the teaching. It probably happened by accident early in my teaching career, but I started telling family stories (about myself, my wife, my children, and now my grandchildren) to illustrate principles in the Christian life. Students especially relish stories that illustrate their teacher (me!) committing a *faux-pas* or embarrassing himself; they can relate to average people, like their professor or common people in history, better than they can to generals and aristocrats. In fact, often these sorts of stories happen to be what alumni fondly remember, and I hope they encourage former students to pursue their own histories and the history of the past. Today we are blessed with books written by great historians such as Stephen Ambrose and David McCullough, who rival Bruce Catton in a story telling style.

James E. Mann, Jr., Mathematics

Flatland
by Edwin A. Abbott

Few books about mathematics have been characterized by their power to expand our theological understanding, and even fewer contain humor or political satire. *Flatland* contains all of this, along with a touch of science fiction, as well. Abbott, writing at the end of the Victorian era, has produced an extended analogy between a two-dimensional flat land and the three-dimensional world in which we live. After giving a vivid and humorous description of Flatland and its inhabitants, he describes the extreme difficulty that one of the inhabitants has in trying to comprehend a being from the three-dimensional world who visits Flatland. In addition to helping young mathematicians comprehend the ideas of dimension higher than three, the analogy will help the young theologian with ideas about God's foreknowledge and predestination. The author gives us a little peek at how God may operate in dimensions that are beyond our comprehension. One final note: Abbott may appear to express a belittling view of women; however, his true view is much higher than that prevailing in the society which he is satirizing.

The Pilgrim's Progress
by John Bunyan

It is possible to do something when you are too young. That has certainly been true for me, and one of things that I did too young was read *Pilgrim's Progress*. I was made to read that book, along with a host of other literary greats, when I was in high school. I'll tell you, I had no love for the book then. However, the aging process caused me to wonder if what I had been required to read as a teenager was really as boring as I remembered. Consequently, as an experiment I have gone back and reread most of my high school reading assignments and discovered that a person's tastes do change. The most marked change was my attitude toward *Pilgrim's Progress*. Bunyan tells *Pilgrim's Progress* as a dream that he has regarding a man named Christian, his wife, and his children. The story, an allegory, is about Christian's travels away from home and his struggles along the way. Many of these struggles are the same ones we face today. Who has not wasted time at Vanity Fair or wallowed in the Slough of Despond? Perhaps I had not been there when I was in high school, but since then I have. The story is a series of vignettes depicting Christian and his fellow travelers at various points of their journey to the City. One of my favorite episodes is when Faithful is overtaken by a man who greets him by knocking him to the ground with his staff. After several rounds of being knocked down, Faithful escapes because another man passes by and bids the first one stop the beating. As Faithful recounts the incident to his friend Christian, Christian tells him that his assailant was Moses and that he "knoweth not how to show mercy to those who transgress His Law." The man who bade Moses stop the beating was the Lord Jesus. What a wonderful picture of how the law beats us down and how we are delivered! Another episode that I have found helpful is the one at the end, when Christian reaches the river and can see the City. He is afraid to cross the raging torrent before him. Bunyan gives a magnificent description of the river to be crossed and the resources God has made available for our crossing. The description has become especially meaningful to me in the last few years, as several of my friends have stood on the banks of the river to say their goodbyes before crossing. In reading the book several times, I have found that proceeding slowly, only one or two episodes per day, is much more satisfying than reading rapidly. The book contains too many illustrations to romp through quickly. Though Bunyan was a tinker by trade and not a writer, the fire in his book, both spiritual and literary, has not been quenched.

Thomas Martin, English

The Life of Samuel Johnson
by James Boswell

To read the 1500 pages of Boswell's *Life of Johnson* is to enjoy one of the great literary experiences. No shortage of accolades has been applied to this work: one of the great books of the Western world, one of the great historical accounts of an age, and the greatest biography ever written. C. S. Lewis said of it that it is rare to read a book and afterwards know the character almost as well as a member of one's family circle. I place the work on my "most influential" list less because it offers a treasury of wisdom and wit and more because it displays the testimony of a highly literate Christian in a highly sophisticated society. Here is a kind of Christianity unfamiliar to us in the early twenty-first century—an august Christianity, one full of intellect and volition, devoid of sentimentality and trite sloganizing. Johnson remains a model of a man who—without wealth, social rank, or political office, but with the gifts given him by God alone—stands in Christian fortitude to use those gifts and make a mark on history. All the while, he raises his stately voice to God's glory rather than his own.

"The Dark" from *The Music School*
"Lifeguard" from *Pigeon Feathers*
by John Updike

More than anything else, two short stories representing Updike's early
short fiction opened my eyes to the power of literature: "The Dark" and
"Lifeguard." As with the best theologically-minded authors–Hawthorne,
Dostoevsky, Milton, and others–there is something Promethean in this
writing. The first time I read these stories I was confronted as never before
with the revelatory force of words, and what a precious and luminescent
gift language really is. "The Dark" is a brief spelunking expedition into the
self, a passing through certain existential terrors associated with twentieth-
century life, as the protagonist ultimately finds rest in his faith. By contrast,
"The Lifeguard" is a story about a person who has been blessed with "too
much light" and squanders it, becoming indulgent and putting his theology
to questionable use. As excited as I've been about Updike's early work,
however, I've also been saddened by much of his middle and later fiction.
Falling from its heights into the sins of the flesh, it offers a kind of limping
aesthetic of sexual promiscuity. Updike once asked, "After Christianity,
what?" Regrettably, his answer: "Sex." Indeed, his words are a striking
commentary on the pathetic substitutions for God wrought by our post-
Christian culture, but they also seem a commentary on his own outlook
and life.

Antigone
by Sophocles

In my estimation, Sophocles' *Antigone* is one of the great dramatic
works from the ancient world that, along with *Oedipus Rex*, has best
stood the test of time. While women were virtually powerless in
Athenian society–and the audience knew, too, that Antigone's father,
Oedipus, had burdened her with an unthinkable ignominy–Antigone
nonetheless stands strong in her conviction of what is right, and not

even the king of the land can dissuade her. She will follow God's law, no matter the cost. Confronting the king, she exclaims, "I did not think your edicts strong enough to overrule the . . . laws of God and heaven, you being only a man. They are not of yesterday or today, but everlasting. . . ." By the end of the play, this powerless woman increases in stature and power, and the authority of the king dwindles to mere ineffectual ranting, till he loses more than he can imagine. All this happens because one woman takes an uncompromising stand on the truth. Those who do not, despite their rank or privilege, come to naught. In Antigone's serene confidence, she proves that the truth is the only solid ground upon which we stand in this world. How many times I have thought of this story and its razor sharp question, dividing so many issues in our lives: Will I obey human laws and do what is expedient, or follow God's law and do what is right? It is the same story told again and again in many great stories through history. One of my favorites from recent years is the Academy-Award winning *Chariots of Fire*, where the main character chooses a path utterly foolish in the world's eyes and seemingly throws away his chance at an Olympic gold medal because he refuses to compromise God's principles. Unique to this story is God's last word on what he thinks about such a person: "I honor those who honor me, says the Lord." For those seeking an uncompromising commitment to Christ in a world opposed to him, much encouragement can be found in these two stories.

Wayne Martindale, English

Wild Swans: Three Daughters of China
by Jung Chang

Sometimes historical events are so strange, so cruel, so comprehensively devastating that a novelist would never dare our credulity with such fantastical happenings; so it is with the century chronicled through the lives of three generations of Chinese women in Jung Chang's historical biography. Beginning in the late nineteenth century, the book presents the author's grandmother, who had the misfortune to be the last in her family to have her feet bound. Through her father's machinations, she becomes one of several concubines of a powerful warlord general, under whom life is first a prison-like isolation, then virtual slavery to the first wife. She escapes to marry a medical man much her senior, and though it is a love match and her husband is kind, the Confucian family order subjects her once again to cruelty. Yet, she and her husband accept poverty over an oppressive family, abandoning the ancestral compound for a hard new life. They then build a new home, surviving into the Japanese conquest of Manchukuo under the puppet emperor Pu Yi (whose story is popularized in the film *The Last Emperor*). The next part of the book focuses on the author's mother, Bao Qin, who represents the next generation. It details Bao's life from her coming of age in the civil war era to the rise and fall of Mao. Although Bao and her husband believe deeply in the Communist movement, willingly undertaking huge sacrifices to advance the cause, they become disillusioned when the system chews them up and Mao unleashes the Cultural Revolution—ten years of anarchy, terror, and destruction. The final section of the book deals with the life of the author herself, Jung Chang, who is born and comes of age during the turbulent Cultural Revolution. Through her eyes we see her parents suffer torture and imprisonment in return for loyalty. We also see the reign of terror subside with Mao's death, and under Deng Xiaoping a new China emerges from isolation, struggling to become a major player in the modern era. Out of this context, Chang, with a combination of brilliant test results and clever maneuvering by her mother, gets the rare opportunity to be educated in England, where she decides to stay. The book ends shortly after the Tiananmen Massacre of June 4, 1989. *Wild Swans* succeeds brilliantly, not only for its human look into a history too bizarre for fiction, but for its look into the human spirit, especially its seemingly boundless capacity for evil, suffering, and endurance. My wife and I have lived and taught in China, which has given us a great love for the Chinese people. We urge others who plan to go there to go prepared; this book will help in doing just that.

The Sweet Everlasting
by Judson Mitcham

One of the most powerful books I've ever read, this recent short novel by Southern Christian writer Judson Mitcham tells a delicate love story from the point of view of a rough-hewn but good-hearted man. At the same time, it offers an unsentimental look into Alzheimer's and the devastation resulting from racism. It ranges from tenderness to terror, from devastation to determination in a mix not unlike Flannery O'Connor. We learn from the first page that the protagonist, Ellis Burt, has just gotten out of prison and has suffered a mental breakdown; we don't learn the reasons for either until the end. The story flashes back briefly to Burt's youth in a sharecropper's family and introduces the black family named Cutts that sharecrop next to them. Burt is independent-minded enough to respect and befriend Otis Cutts, who is the same age. The story jumps quickly to Burt's rescue of a young woman named Susan from two ruffians at the fair where Burt runs the Tilt-A-Whirl. Susan thanks Burt for saving her by threatening to bust his head open with a rock. From this unlikely beginning, Burt and Susan develop a relationship, marry, and have a son. With painful irony, this beautifully developed family relationship survives temptation, only to explode, ironically, over racial issues. On the way to its arresting climax, Mitcham constantly surprises us, stripping back the layers of history, culture, personal experience, prejudice, and strength that bring Burt's story to a gut-wrenching crescendo. By the end, the story left me stunned at the magnitude of self-inflicted human suffering.

Rani V. Mathai, Education

Death of a Guru
by Rabi R. Maharaj

For the past two thousand years believers have heard stories of the transforming power of the Gospel of Jesus Christ. Every conversion narrative is unique, encouraging the faithful to spread the good news. This story inspired me when I read it a few years ago. *Death of a Guru* is an autobiography of a Brahmin priest who converted to the Christian faith. In his story, Rabi Maharaj, who descended from a long line of Brahmin priests and gurus, describes the struggles and disillusionment he felt even after the careful observance of the Hindu customs, rituals for "moksha," and training as a yogi. His was a difficult search for the meaning of life, and his choice between Hinduism and Christ involved serious challenges. But when he finally encountered Jesus, the result was a triumph over death—"through the death of a guru." The title itself has a threefold meaning: it points to the death of Maharaj's father, a practicing guru who had taken a vow of silence; it points to Maharaj's own death unto self as a Hindu guru, which happened once he met the Lord; and it points to the death of THE GURU, Jesus Christ. This book is especially insightful at a time when Eastern mysticism and philosophy are competing with the claims of Christ.

Cry, the Beloved Country
by Alan Paton

Cry, the Beloved Country is the profoundly compassionate story of the Zulu pastor Stephen Kumalo and his son Absalom, set against the backdrop of the lovely landscape of South Africa, a land torn apart by racial inequality and injustice. Paton's gripping narrative still remains as the best known novel in the history of South Africa. It portrays, with full gravity, the struggle of life in a country oppressed by apartheid. All the characters, interestingly, possess a clear understanding of their situations. *Cry, the Beloved Country* remains a classic tale because of the timelessness and universality of its dialogues conveying the emotions and tensions of a deprived people, living in terror in their own native land. Paton has succeeded in making his readers aware of the reality of the evil that mars human culture, and in inspiring a renewed faith in the dignity of the human race. Ultimately, this represents yet another tale of the Fall and the Redemption. Two years ago my son chose this book for a reading project in school. As a family, we decided to read and to discuss the book together. It pleased my husband and me to hear our boys talking about the tensions of the characters in the book; our sons' sense of justice and compassion were aroused. Above all, we rejoiced in the moving message of unconditional forgiveness, which we all agreed is the only hope for the human race.

How Now Shall We Live?
by Charles Colson and Nancy Pearcey

This book was given to me as a graduation gift by a friend. Chuck Colson and Nancy Pearcey, in their book, *How Now Shall We Live?*, present Christianity as a "total worldview and life system." Their goal is to bring the message of partnership with God, all in an effort to build a new Christian culture in a world full of conflicting worldviews. In the first part of the book they explain the term "worldview." In the subsequent parts they compare and contrast the various ideas and philosophies that compete to explain the basic questions of human existence. Such questions include the following: "Where did we come from and who are we? What has gone wrong with the world? What can we do to fix it?" Taking examples from politics, education, and the arts, the authors expose the flaws of the materialistic worldview and provide a coherent worldview based on the Bible, challenging our generation to discern the times. Theories and examples from all disciplines are written in the language of lay people; furthermore, the reading is made easier through stories and illustrations. The authors were inspired primarily by the Scriptures and by the works of great Christian writers and philosophers. Excellent notes, a "further reading list," and vivid stories that illustrate abstract principles–these are some of the special features of this worthwhile book. For the members of a Christian college community, this book is especially useful because its central theme is the integration of faith and learning and living.

Brooke McLaughlin, English

In the Name of Jesus
by Henri J. M. Nouwen

Nouwen's *In the Name of Jesus* is one of those very small books that makes good use of its space. It was small enough to fit into my backpack when I worked as a camp counselor, trying to minister to mentally handicapped campers and struggling to figure out my own place in this changing world. Through that summer, I found myself returning again and again–as I have continued since–to the insight of Nouwen. Nouwen's message, regarding the centrality and nature of God in our lives and the way that centrality translates into our responsibility to our greater community, was much needed, and it served as a grounding for me during this time of turmoil in my life. The book grows out of Nouwen's work with the L'Arche community of mentally handicapped people. As he ministered to them, he found that in many ways, ironically, they were ministering to him. The central message of *In the Name of Jesus*–"Are you in love with Jesus?"–grows into a recognition of our calling as believers. We are called to be servants, and we are not called into this service alone. The path that Nouwen outlines is a simple one; instead of desiring to *do* for God, he asserts that we must desire to be *in* God. The doing will naturally follow. The other emphasis in Nouwen's thoughts is on how this doing unites us with those around us, and on the importance of those relationships. The doing that grows through being is done only through interaction with others, whether they are people we lead, or people who lead us; in either case, we should see the worth in those individuals and our relationships with them.

Phyllis Mitchell, Foreign Languages

The Adventures of Don Quixote
by Miguel de Cervantes Saavedra

Among the many reasons I recommend Miguel de Cervantes' *Don Quixote of the Mancha,* I mention only two: first, it teaches me about reading; and second, its main character is unforgettable. Because *Quixote* is long–even small print volumes run to a thousand pages–many people never open it. But in the first words of the prologue, Cervantes gives us an invaluable lesson about the nature of reading, beginning with the curious and precisely chosen words "Idle reader. . . ." Truly, it is written for the reader who has time, who is, in a literal sense, "idle." To be anything less is to do disservice to the book. Why? Much of the humor and delight is lost to the hurried reader. Therefore, *Quixote* can only be read *well* at the pace of a few pages at a time–a pace that reminds us that reading is an experience to be savored. Secondly, don Quixote is a brilliant, almost archetypal, character. What dedicated reader cannot help but laugh at a man who has been driven mad by reading novels? This is only one of many aspects of his nature that slyly force us to laugh at ourselves, too. Likewise, he functions as a powerful reminder that our true accomplishments don't always look the way we expect them to and that a little down-to-earth madness is essential for getting anything *really* important done.

The Road from Coorain
by Jill Ker Conway

The Road from Coorain, by Jill Ker Conway, is the first part of a modern adventure story in which the young heroine struggles against considerable odds to leave the terrible, yet incredibly beautiful, Australian outback as well as a family and society unaccustomed to the idea that a woman should be given the opportunity for outstanding achievement. She eventually becomes a well-known historian and even the first woman president of Smith College. I like this book because, like many professional women who grew up in the mid-twentieth century, I keenly felt the lack of adequate role models in the professional world I had worked so hard to enter. Indeed, many women today still face formidable challenges in achieving their professional goals. This extremely well-written memoir gives me (and no doubt other readers who face obstacles in fulfilling their goals) a sense of having company, largely through the vicarious difficulties of the author's individual journey. I would also recommend this book to male colleagues in academia who may still be wondering "why women make such a fuss."

Douglas Moo,
Biblical and Theological Studies

Mere Christianity
by C. S. Lewis

This Lewis classic was the first book I read after becoming a Christian as a senior in college in 1971. I have always been thankful for God's grace in leading me to this book. In his characteristic lucid prose, Lewis presents a compelling case for what J. R. W. Stott has called "BBC" . . . Basic, balanced Christianity. *Mere Christianity* is not the most sophisticated apologetic for the Christian faith that one can find. But it was precisely what I needed when I first read it: a simple description and defense of the Christian worldview. In thirty years of Christian experience, theological study and ministry of various kinds, I have added many personal convictions about Scripture, God, and the world to Lewis' basic Christian characteristics. But reading Lewis early on, coming on top of a college academic career that was explicitly pagan, instilled in me a sense for the essence of the faith and a distrust of those who would insist that their version of the faith is the only legitimate one. Our current pluralistic climate confronts Christians with two opposite temptations. The siren voice of toleration tempts us to reduce the essence of the faith so as to admit as many professing Christians as possible: the "big tent" approach. But overreaction to the climate of our times is also a danger. We may begin drawing the boundaries of true Christianity too narrowly, giving creedal status to our own theological visions. Lewis does not draw the lines perfectly (who could?), but his very approach brings needed perspective in our attempt to defend a "mere" Christian worldview.

The Literature of England, Volume II
by George K. Anderson and William E. Buckler (Editors)

This volume was the single textbook for a course in English poetry that I took during my junior year in college. As a political science major, I took the course only because 1) I needed a course in this area, 2) the time slot fit my schedule, and 3) the professor had a good reputation as a lecturer. As advocates of liberal arts education will be happy to hear, I got more than I ever dreamed of from the course. Always a voracious reader, my tastes had run to classic prose literature, historical novels, and (yes) a whole gamut of modern "escapist" novels. I am not sure that I had ever read a poem with any serious attention. But Wordsworth changed all that. Since the class began with the romantics, Wordsworth was one of the first poets we encountered. And the excerpts we read from *The Prelude* awakened in me a sense of nature and subjective experience that had lain dormant all my life. My interest in the volume turned quickly from the pragmatic (read to pass tests) to the aesthetic (read for enjoyment). I read more than was assigned and discovered other poets who also captured my imagination in a way that I had not thought possible, including Coleridge's *Kubla Khan* and Matthew Arnold's *Dover Beach*. What impact this aesthetic awakening had on my conversion to Christianity, only eight months later, is difficult to determine. But, in retrospect, I think a relationship may exist. My education and inclinations had instilled in me a rather rationalistic approach to my own life. The English poetry I read created in me a longing for an imaginative world or experience that would transcend the world susceptible to rational description (I think here of Lewis' *Surprised by Joy*). God, I now believe, prepared me through my love of some of the English poets for an encounter with the One who has created and fulfills all our aesthetic longing.

Gregory Morrison, Library Science

Way of the Ascetics
by Tito Colliander
(Translated by Katharine Ferre)

For most of Christianity in the West, the knowledge and practice of ascetic spiritual disciplines have been lost and forgotten. Colliander, an Orthodox lay person from Finland, reminds us that Christianity is and has always been an ascetic religion. The Lord explicitly calls his followers to a life of self-denial if they would follow him. This little book helps define the substance and the manner of this ascetic way of life and the purpose it fulfills. Based on "direct or freely rendered extracts" from the Church fathers, *Way of the Ascetics* offers the "Western reader something of the atmosphere of Orthodox spirituality," according to Kenneth Leech, an Anglican priest who writes the excellent introduction to the book. It provides the proper context for understanding and appropriating what follows. The first several chapters focus on the necessity of recognizing the depth of our self-will and our "immoderately high faith of ourselves." Later chapters concentrate principally on the theme of prayer, the premier and most essential ascetic labor. The book's general tone may strike you as excessive and gloomy. Nevertheless, Colliander anticipates the reader's response: "You are perhaps wondering, is this really necessary? The holy Fathers reply with another question: Do you really think that you can fill a jar with clean water before the old, dirty water has been emptied out? . . . No, he who hopes to see the Lord as he is, purifies himself, says the Apostle John." This book has been a great encouragement to me in the struggle to pray; yet, it also is a source of discontent because of my double-mindedness. It stands as a constant reminder that I can't have both worlds or serve two masters. The way of life set forth in Colliander's work epitomizes for me G. K. Chesterton's "Christian ideal" when he wrote, "The Christian ideal has not been tried and found wanting; it has been found difficult and left untried."

From the Holy Mountain: A Journey Among the Christians of the Middle East
by William Dalrymple

From the Holy Mountain is a brilliantly conceived and fashioned account of William Dalrymple's trek across the Middle East in 1994. Intrigued by a popular Byzantine travel memoir from the early seventh century, Dalrymple follows in the footsteps of its author, John Moschos, to witness firsthand "Christianity's devastating decline in the land of its birth."

Dalrymple sees the writing on the wall already in the book written by this wandering Christian monk, the *Spiritual Meadow*. But by the end of the book, the reader comes away with much more than a report of the now desperate conditions for the predominantly Orthodox Christians there. As Dalrymple shares the many tales of his personal journey, he also takes us to school in the subjects of Church history, ancient and Byzantine art, and world politics, to mention just a few areas he is competent to address. Add to this mix his exceptional writing ability, and the effect is as satisfying as it is unsettling. For many of us, our perceptions about the Middle East are built solely on the nightly news reports. *From the Holy Mountain* provides a welcome corrective to many of our assumptions and an escape from our general ignorance. I recommend this book to anyone, but the overall impact of the book will be greater for the Christian reader, who is left to contemplate the meaning and impact of a dying Christian civilization in the Middle East. This book has influenced me considerably in the way I perceive the current situation in the Middle East, as well as the historic relationship between Muslims and Christians. Dalrymple has led me to contemplate the great mystery of life together on this planet.

Sally Morrison,
Education

Let Your Life Speak:
Listening to the Voice of Vocation
by Parker Palmer

There are several authors, especially in the field of education, whose works I follow closely. The more I meet with them through their books, the more I feel I am casually conversing with friends: I am anxious to hear their opinions, and they are ready to respond to my questions. Once in a great while, authors risk making themselves transparent to their readers as they reveal both highlights and lowlights of their personal experience. These glimpses into the hearts and minds of authors enable us to understand how both the chilly winters and the warm summer seasons of their experience have sparked the embers of thought, igniting the very words that become crystallized treasures to their readers. Such is the case with the author Parker Palmer. While several of Palmer's works explore the spiritual dimension of human relationships in teaching, it is his most recent book that reveals the author's personal journey and response to vocation. In *Let Your Life Speak*, Palmer describes vocation as an *inner voice* that calls the individual to listen and respond to the true self God has created that person to be. He describes the paradoxes that emerge throughout the seasons of his vocational journey as he learns, in one memorable line, to be "comfortable in one's own skin without wearing other people's faces."

Families Where Grace Is in Place
by Jeff VanVonderven

I was struck by this title in one of my bookstore-browsing sessions. As I seek to grow in my understanding of the transforming power of God's grace, I realize the importance of taking a periodic inventory, a *barometric read*, of my many family relationships: those in my immediate family, as a spouse and mother; in my church family, as a sister in Christ; and in my professional family, as a teacher and professional peer. Considering the many family circles we are in, what exactly should grace look like in our relationships? VanVonderven answers that question as he provides a framework to examine our motives and interactions. Especially illuminating are the numerous examples he provides of *curse-filled* relationships: those in which the destructive power of misplaced identity and the misuse of Scripture are used as a means of controlling others. He then contrasts those with examples of *grace-filled* relationships: only living *by the Book* and allowing the Holy Spirit to work in us can heal us from within so we can live in right relationship with those around us.

That's Not What I Meant: How Conversational Style Makes or Breaks Relationships
by Deborah Tannen

The field of linguistics is often discussed in highly theoretical terms, rarely giving a reader practical information on how people use language in their everyday lives. Tannen is one linguist, however, who conveys insights gleaned from her research in language easily understood by even the novice reader. She describes how communication not only includes the meanings of our words, but also our *metamessages* or attitudes about our relationships we convey along with our words. These metamessages are what individuals react to most in conversation, she says, less so the words. The consequences can be positive or negative: they can either make or break a relationship. I have found Tannen's descriptions of conversational styles helpful in my own building of congruent communication with others. Her book has also helped bring to light the frames and boundaries embedded throughout my acts of personal and professional communication.

Mark A. Noll,
History

Chronicles of Wasted Time
by Malcolm Muggeridge

This is a great book, although exactly what kind of great book is hard to say. Muggeridge presented this two-volume work as an autobiography, but the books are selective to the point of fiction, and strongly backloaded to reflect Muggeridge's opinions as they had come to develop by the 1970s. Doubts as to genre notwithstanding, the volumes are as crisp an evisceration of the modern *Zeitgeist* as one could possibly hope to read. Muggeridge knew almost everyone of note in Britain and also in many other places of the world. As told here, his life was a perpetual series of disillusionments with the gods of the age–Fabianism, Marxist socialism, Western affluence. Even more, his life proved to be a progressive self-understanding of what it meant, as a journalist extraordinaire (even in the most secular of centuries), to be haunted by God. The more I find out about the real Malcolm Muggeridge, the less I am sure about recommending his character. (He was particularly suspect in becoming a loud critic as an old man of sins he had himself simply outgrown.) Doubts about his person notwithstanding, this two-volume work points people in the right direction because it points them to God.

The Missionary Movement in Christian History: Studies in the Transmission of Faith
by Andrew Walls

This must be the best book ever written to show how the world-wide spread of Christianity fulfills the inner character of the Incarnation. As a series of essays, the volume suffers some from occasional repetition and a few gaps of coverage, but these are minor blemishes compared to the riches it unfolds. Walls argues that Christianity, in its essence, is a religion of translation—first the Word of God into human flesh, then Jewish forms of Christian faith into Mediterranean, then Mediterranean into Northern European, then Northern European into the diverse cultures to the ends of the earth. By studying the process of translation—by noting the often very different ways in which Christianity takes root in different cultures at different times—believers can marvel at how God so creatively combines the eternal and timeless with the time-bound and parochial. The result is a theology of culture and of Christian mission true to "the Word made flesh." It does not hurt the impact of the book that Walls is as witty as he is humble, and that his scholar's eye can synthesize telling details from the whole length of Christian history with the whole breadth of modern Christian expansion.

The Parting of Friends: The Wilberforces and Henry Manning
by David Newsome

Newsome's multiple biography is an old-fashioned kind of history about old-fashioned kind of people. His subjects lived in the luminous circle created by the household of William Wilberforce, in the first half of the nineteenth century. This circle was made up of several of Wilberforce's children, their friends and colleagues, and their sisters' and sisters' friends—themselves a remarkable group of Victorian women. The plot line is the story of the drift from the sturdy evangelicalism of the older Wilberforce to high church Anglicanism and then, for some under the guidance of John Henry Newman, to the Roman Catholic church. The poignancy of the story is the combination of intense fraternal devotion and painful ecclesiastical separation. When some in this circle remained Anglican, the result was broken relationships in homes, colleges (most were connected to Oxford), and the church. Newsome's gift is to shape the treasure trove of letters left by the participants (they were scribbling away *all* the time) into a compelling narrative that, while it solves no problems of theology or church-loyalty, nonetheless demonstrates the profound humanity of those who engaged those issues in that corner of Victorian England a century and a half ago.

William (Mary Anne) Phemister, Conservatory of Music

The Dean's Watch
by Elizabeth Goudge

I love to read life-changing stories about extraordinary people. After I found my first Elizabeth Goudge novel, *A Bird in the Tree*, I was captivated by her storytelling spell. Somehow, she has been overlooked, as evidenced by the following: rarely seeing her books anywhere, not finding her death date (1984) in library catalogs, and noting her absence from commentaries about twentieth-century British writers. With more than forty-five books written (including *Green Dolphin Street*, which was turned into a 1947 MGM Academy Award-winning film), hers is not an inconsequential output. *The Dean's Watch* is, for me, the most moving and deeply personal of all her novels. Reading this work encouraged my calling of teaching young apprentices. I experienced, away from my piano, the joys of creating something both useful and uniquely artistic. Faith animates every page Goudge writes. And in this book her characters are all significantly locked into their fallen behavior, seemingly without hope for change: an atheist appears closer to God than the Dean of the Cathedral; children live in poverty, orphanages, or dull apprenticeships with little, if any, prospect for a meaningful future; women suffer through joyless marriages and become bitter because they, in fact, have no marriage at all. But eventually change does occur. In all Goudge's writing, her virtuoso technique of anthropomorphism leaves the reader with no doubt about what dogs, cats, birds, and trees happen to think about. Her fiction even presents us with timepieces that have souls and can affect the way we feel about life and eternity. (After reading Goudge, I won't be able to think about my digital watch in quite the same way again!) [Reviewed by William.]

No Time for Silence:
Evangelical Women in Public Ministry
Around the Turn of the Century
by Janette Hassey

Professor Edith Blumhofer introduced me to Janette Hassey's *No Time for Silence* when I took her course in Women in Ministry in 1987. This well-documented study of women in ministry between 1880 and 1930 encouraged my fundamentalist-reared heart. With astonishing regularity Hassey uncovered information that confounded the myth that believers with a high view of scripture (even inerrancy) must dispute the legitimacy of women in ministry. The evidence unearthed in the archives of the early Bible institutes (especially Moody) and multiple denominational records dashed the assumption that the feminist movement among evangelicals is merely a misguided effort influenced by secular feminism since the 1950s. Documentation abounds for the early endorsement of women's public ministry in all areas of Christian service. The book also illuminates how the present prohibitions to women in ministry developed. The historical accounts of dedicated men and women contained in this book, all committed to using and heartily endorsing the public gifts of women in the church, enlivened my soul with hope. [Reviewed by Mary Anne.]

Pattle Pun,
Biology

Intelligent Design:
The Bridge between Science and Theology
by William Dembski

William Dembski has produced a masterpiece expounding the controversial model of Intelligent Design (ID) for the educated Christian layperson and open-minded seeker. He divides his book into three parts: "The Historical Backdrop," "A Theory of Design," and "Bridging Science and Theology." Part One surveys the traditional apologetic arguments of "sign," "miracles," and, among others, the development and the demise of British Natural Theology. In Dembski's second part, "A Theory of Design," he develops the model of Intelligent Design by providing it with two criteria: the Complexity-Specification Criterion from information theory, and the Irreducible Complexity Principle from biology. In Dembski's final part, he attempts to relate theology to science by proposing a mutual support model using the analogy that pilots in airplanes, approaching mountains at different heights, may have different but mutually supportive perspectives of the same reality. He develops a logical argument of explanatory power of the Design model based on its consonance, contribution, and champion among competing explanations. Finally, claiming Christ as the *telos* of God's creation, he attempts to put Christ back into the sciences to complete the holistic view of Christology. In the Appendices of the book, Dembski attempts to respond to various criticisms of the ID movement. The introduction of the ID concept allows alternative explanations of scientific observations to be explored. It does not limit scientific investigation, but rather encourages it by looking at more alternatives. The insistence that there is no gap in natural events is the major premise of Naturalism, which, to most contemporary thinkers, has failed to account for reality. In my opinion, Dembski's book is perfect for thoughtful readers interested in science and faith issues. It presents the ID movement in an intelligible and yet thoroughly defensible context. The book shows us that biologists are debating the mechanisms of evolution under the Darwinian paradigm; however, new insights cannot be fostered in this debate if the naturalistic paradigm is the only permissible presupposition. It has become increasingly recognized among biologists that the gradualistic process of Darwinian selection (*microevolution*) fails to account for the major features of developmental changes above the species level (*macroevolution*). Although the naturalistic assumption has proven to be fruitful in the realm of "Operation Science," the ID movement may allow us to break new ground in the pursuit of "Origin Science," which from my perspective is a necessary development.

Darwin's Black Box: The Biochemical Challenge to Evolution
by Michael Behe

For over a century and a half, the Darwinian paradigm of gradualistic evolution has dominated biological science as the only acceptable model for the origins of diversity. Mutations selected by favorable environments allow organisms carrying such mutations to multiply and take over niches. Variations within populations, as well as speciation (so-called microevolution) are well explained by Darwinian Natural Selection. However, Darwinian mechanisms are hard pressed to explain the origin of features at high taxa. Michael Behe has brought this problem of diversity to the molecular level. Bio-chemically speaking, molecular machines–for example, cilium, bacterial flagellum, the blood coagulation cascade, self-defense on the cellular level, and the intricate cellular system required to make its "building blocks"–are models for Irreducible

Complexity (IC). Under conditions where all things being equal, IC is defined by Behe as "a single system composed of several well-matched, interacting parts that contribute to the basic function, wherein the removal of any one of the parts causes the system to effectively cease functioning. An irreducibly complex system cannot be produced directly (that is, by continuously improving the initial function, which continues to work by the same mechanism) by slight, successive modifications of a precursor system, because any precursor to an irreducibly complex system that is missing a part is by definition nonfunctional." Behe suggests that the model systems he describes are irreducibly complex, and therefore challenge Darwinian evolution at the core of its mechanism. As Darwin once remarked, "If it could be demonstrated that any complex organ existed which could not possibly have been formed by numerous, successive, slight modification, my theory would absolutely break apart." While it is debatable whether all of his model systems are irreducibly complex, Behe nonetheless focuses our attention on one of the most perplexing problems in modern biology, namely, the origins of integrated molecular systems. Intelligent Design may actually be a better alternative paradigm under which future theorizing and experimentation on the studies of origins can be carried out, i.e., examination of the *minimal* components of an integrated unit, rather than searching for gradualistic transition from precursors that may turn out to be non-existent. The scientific world will be much impoverished if such consideration is ruled out merely on the basis of philosophical commitment to naturalism.

Paul Robinson,
Human Needs and Global Resources

For All God's Worth
by N. T. Wright

During more than four decades of living and working in the *Two-Thirds World*, I witnessed and struggled with many things: the challenges of poverty in the slums of Nairobi; ecological disaster and hunger in the famine camps of Ethiopia and Somalia; conflict and genocide in Rwanda; racial prejudice and injustice in South Africa; and AIDS in East Africa. In these and other situations, my experiences have been that Christians are fundamentally divided on the purpose and mission of the church in a broken and hurting world. In a deeply reflective and challenging little book, *For All God's Worth*, N. T. Wright invites the people of God to consider what is their central calling. Wright centers his essays on the theme of "worship" derived from "worth-ship," which literally means giving God all he is worth. True and unadulterated worship derived from a clear vision of God's greatness and love, Wright argues, must lead into total and unwavering *mission*al service to a world in desperate need of reconciliation and healing. Through an image of the cross, incarnated in the people of God, Wright envisions the church as standing with arms outstretched, holding onto Christ and his cross with one hand and to those we are given to love with the other. For what purpose? Wright explains, "so that the healing love of Christ may flow out into the world, to confront violence and injustice with the rebuke of the cross, and to comfort the injured and wronged with the consolation of the cross."

Jerry Root,
Christian Formation and Ministry

Barchester Towers
by Anthony Trollope

Barchester Towers is a Victorian novel set in the bishopric of Barset. The characters of the story are primarily the clergymen and their family members, intimately involved in the religious life of the region. Most memorable is the Reverend Septimus Harding, formerly the Warden of Hiram's Hospital. He is a principled man, unique in his world. While many men of principle are quick to reference their own standards as a means for judging the scruples of others, Harding finds greater profit in the scrutinizing of his own behavior and shortcomings. Nothing of the busybody in him, he is full of humility and gentleness. The same cannot be said of his son-in-law, the Reverend Doctor Grantly, whose life is full of crusades. Whether those causes are kingdom-worthy, the reader will have to decide, but one thing is clear: many of his crusades are designed chiefly to protect the interests of Dr. Grantly. Then there is Eleanor Bold, the young but widowed daughter of Rev. Harding. She is a woman of excellence, principled like her father, with good boundaries, making her unlikely to be manipulated by anyone. The Bishop's chaplain is Reverend Obadiah Slope, whom, Trollope promptly inserts, only recently added the "E" to his last name. So pretentious and self-serving is this man that we readily discover his whole life consists of adding "E"s to things in the hopes of making them look better than they are. Unforgettable are Bishop and Mrs. Proudie, the Stanhopes, the large family of Rev. Quiverful, the intelligent (and kind) Mr. Arabin. Even characters who appear briefly are, in their way, memorable; the lawyer Mr. Vellum Deeds and the Doctors Sir Lamda Mewnew and Sir Omicron Pie. What proves to be most fascinating to me about this novel, and the reason I read it time and again, is that Trollope weaves various character types together into a tapestry. This colorful fabric provides the reader with a kind of map for making sense of the complex interactions of persons, which is so much a part of life's topography. The characters portrayed fall into four categories, as I see it: goofy people who know they are goofy, and thus are able to live with a certain degree of honesty; goofy people who do not know they are goofy, and thus are dangerous; goofy people who are aware that they are goofy but want no one else to know it, and thus lean toward being pretentious; and goofy people who know they are goofy, but remain too lazy to care or change. Indeed, we are a goofy lot—and, as a believer, I think it is good to remember that this is so! *Barchester Towers* is a novel that never lets us forget this truth.

Pensées
by Blaise Pascal

There are many reasons why I am attracted to the writing of the seventeenth-century French philosopher and physicist, Blaise Pascal. You cannot live a day of your life without being somehow affected by his life–his work. When you hear a weather report, remember that he invented the barometer. When you step on the brakes in your car, be grateful he was the father of the science of hydraulics. When you use a computer or a calculator, remember that he invented the first calculating machine and for that reason has been called the father of the modern computer. (In fact, a computer language, *Pascal*, was named in his honor.) He is the father of the science of probability, he developed the first public transportation system, and his *Provincial Letters* are to the French language what Shakespeare is to English. His genius has been compared with that of Plato, Aristotle, Augustine, da Vinci, and Galileo. On November 23, 1654, at thirty-one, Pascal converted to Christianity. He set out to write a lengthy work in Christian apologetics, recording his thoughts on scraps of paper. When he was thirty-nine he took a poor family suffering from small pox off the streets of Paris and into his home. Tragically, Pascal contracted the disease himself and died suddenly. Yet after his death, his sister Jacqueline, a Jansenist nun, organized the scraps and fragments of her brother's unfinished apology into what is now known as the *Pensées*. It is a book full of thoughts so elegant, even its lack of completion could not prevent its publication. The work, broken up into short passages, is full of truths so clear and opinions so reasonable that they appear almost axiomatic; each is worthy of deeper reflection and further application. Frankly, I cannot read the *Pensées* (which translated simply means *thoughts*) and remain intellectually idle, nor is it possible for my heart to remain passive. Pascal himself wrote, "The heart has its reasons that reason does not know." This fact does not encourage either sloppy thinking or mediocrity; it simply acknowledges that all is not accessible to reason. He wrote, "The last proceeding of reason is to recognize that there is an infinity of things which are beyond it. It is but feeble if it does not see so far as to know this. But if natural things are beyond it, what will be said of supernatural?" While Pascal delights in reason, he enjoys much, much more: "If we submit everything to reason, our religion will be absurd and ridiculous." He takes the supernatural and metaphysical seriously, which comes as a breath of fresh air to an age like our own, dominated by materialism. But Pascal equally delights in a faith that makes sense, also a refreshing change in an age when so much religious thought is full of nonsense. He writes that "there are two kinds of people one can call reasonable: those who serve God with all their heart because they know Him, and those who seek Him with all their heart because they do not know Him." This is a book worthy to be read many times over the course of a life.

Erwin P. Rudolph,
English

A History of the English Language
by Albert C. Baugh and Thomas Cable

This invaluable book is one to which I have returned again and again for an in-depth account of how the English language has developed to its present state. It is challenging reading for even the advanced student, but it can be readily understood and enjoyed in its major outlines by the average reader. It gives some attention to the development of sounds and inflections of the language, as well as to the political, social, and intellectual forces in the different historical periods that helped determine the course of the language's development. The author convinces us that the sound basis for understanding and appreciating present-day English is "a knowledge and understanding of the path it has pursued in becoming what it is."

Orthodoxy
by G. K. Chesterton

Through Chesterton's *Orthodoxy* I have been moved to look anew at the world about me with open-eyed wonder. I have seen in it a fresh emphasis upon imagination, adventure, and romance. As a searcher for truth, the author is struck by what he discovers beyond mere logic in a world of poetical curiosity. As he insists, "How much happier you would be . . . if the hammer of a higher God could smash your small cosmos, scattering the stars like spangles, and leave you in the open, free like other men to took up as well as down." Hence, we should never assume that such events as the sunrise and sunset just happen with daily monotonous regularity, but review them as a "dramatic encore." God "did it again" by daily divine intervention! The same is true for other wonders in the world in which we live.

Paradise Lost
by John Milton

John Milton stands out among the seventeenth-century poets as one who not only adhered to the classical ideal of delighting and instructing, but as one who never forgot that his talent for poetry was God-given. Here is one poet who set before himself the lifelong aim of producing for the world a *magnum opus* that would be the capstone of his poetical achievement. The result was an epic poem in blank verse depicting the whole situation in which man finds himself and how his situation came to be. *Paradise Lost* is the greatest epic in the English language—one that is rich and varied in its artistic achievement and one that maintains its high poetical level throughout with remarkable facility and ease. The demands it makes upon the concentration of the modern reader will be amply rewarded by the imaginative embellishments it provides for the biblical account.

Ewan Russell, Kinesiology

Experiencing the Depths of Jesus Christ
by Jeanne Guyon

Imagine reading a book that was publicly burned in France for its perceived heretical Christian teachings in the seventeenth century. Or what about reading a book that has been kept from general public reading for nearly three hundred years, perhaps because it contains a few of the highest insights and deepest revelations of the secrets of *experiencing* Christ that have ever been penned? This is the book—it is, in my opinion, a "pearl of great price" or a "treasure hidden in a field." Other than the Bible, no book has been more instrumental in my life than this relatively short, straight forward and personal accounting of how to turn and yield your heart to the Lord—how to make that a gift to Him. I came across this book a few years ago, quite by accident, when I was wanting a deeper relationship with God. The insights that Guyon expressed revolutionized my prayer life. Now my encounter with Him in all of life is more heart-felt. Christ is embraced not only in my mind, but more importantly, He is embraced in a consuming encounter. How then does one turn and yield one's heart to the Lord, that is, how can one know Him in a deep way? Guyon suggests that a certain kind of prayer that is very simple and yet holds the key to perfection and goodness is the means one can use to ultimately find union with God. That this book has been brought to your attention may be an indication that God wants to do a special work in your heart.

The Evidential Power of Beauty
by Thomas Dubay

As an anatomy professor, I know well the beauty and wonder of the human body. Despite the messiness when dissecting a cadaver, the words "fearfully and wonderfully made" often echo in my brain as I work on one—I can see real beauty here. So it was my deep appreciation for the beauty of the human body that led me to this powerful and comprehensive treatise on a theology of beauty. Every normal person knows what beauty is, says Dubay, even though few can define its meaning. In this book beauty is examined on the sense level, just as one would admire glittering diamonds in a jewelry store. It is also examined on a spiritual level, such as appreciating brilliant poetry or the radiance of a pure and saintly soul. Finally, it is examined on a divine level, which is to appreciate the beauty of God. If there is a primary thesis, I believe it is *that one can recognize truth by its beauty and simplicity.* That both science and theology are coming to this realization is a major theme. What I like most about this book is the attention that Dubay gives to the phenomenal beauty and detail of creation. One is left ultimately with only one conclusion–that there had to be a Designer. For example, talking about the fifty billion galaxies in our universe, Dubay quotes the astronomer Chet Raymo, who says, "I have often made a model of a spiral galaxy on the floor with a box of salt. It would take 10,000 boxes of salt to have as many grains in the model as there are stars in the Andromeda Galaxy!" Who dare say there is no God? The evidence, as Dubay shares it, is overwhelming.

Leland Ryken, English

Mere Christianity
by C. S. Lewis

In general, the books that were most influential in my life were ones that I encountered during my college and graduate school education. *Mere Christianity* crossed my path sometime during my undergraduate years, though I do not remember under what circumstances. Several aspects of the book captured me and have continued to make it one of the great and influential books in my life. One is the British logic by which Lewis plays with a topic, turning it like a prism in the light and lending validition to his conclusions. Another is the liveliness of the style, especially its conversational quality and the effectiveness of its analogies and metaphors. Those qualities of the book are what have made it captivating to me, but the thing that has made it influential in my life is the way in which it clarifies Christian morality and doctrine, making them both logically convincing and appealing. The effect of reading Lewis' accounts of the Christian virtues is to make me want to practice them. Also, I have always found reassuring the many points at which this obviously scholarly author is so awake to ordinary experience.

"An Apology for Poetry" (1595)
by Sir Philip Sidney

"Of Education" (1644)
by John Milton

These two Renaissance essays are "classic texts" that can be found, respectively, in virtually any anthology of sixteenth-century literature and edition of Milton's works. Although I first read these essays in graduate school, their true importance in my life began during the first year or two of my teaching at Wheaton (to which I came immediately after graduate school). Like many classic texts from the past, these essays require the best effort from a reader today, but they will repay whatever one invests in them. The influence of the essays on me stems from the way in which they say in kernel form virtually all that I would most want to say about the integration of literature and Christianity (Sidney) and Christian liberal arts education (Milton). As I have written on those two subjects through the years, these are the foundational texts. Comprehensiveness of vision characterizes both essays, which cover (briefly but in a well-thought-out manner) all the essential dimensions of literature and education. For me these treatises remain a never-failing fountain of insight on two of the subjects that have most concerned me as a Christian scholar and teacher.

Fundamentalism and the Word of God
by J. I. Packer

The criterion of a book's being influential is not exactly the same as the criterion of a book's greatness. Influential books are influential partly because of the time they enter our lives. Thus, while few would rank Packer's book *Fundamentalism and the Word of God* quite on a par with several of his subsequent books, it is nonetheless the Packer book that has been the most influential in my life. I found and purchased the book–paperback form–in a small Christian bookstore in a small Iowa town during my sophomore year in college. I underlined it. I pondered it. I was influenced by it. The British flavor, the meticulousness of documentation, the attention to the logic of the argument, and the organizing mentality were winsome to me. But the influence stemmed primarily from the fact that this was the first time I had fully confronted the case for the reliability of the Bible as God's guide for life. I have never gone back and reread the book in its entirety, and I have only occasionally referred to it. I have not needed to do so. The important thing for me is that I remember that the case for the reliability of the Bible as the final authority for belief is firm. Packer's book fostered my abiding confidence in Scripture.

Alan D. Savage,
Foreign Languages

Madame Bovary
by Gustave Flaubert

I have been carrying *Madame Bovary* around with me ever since I first read it as a graduate student. Not physically, of course, but as some sort of permanent fixture in my interior landscape. I say "some sort" because I'm not sure that I can explain all the reasons this novel has had such an impact on me. I can, nonetheless, explain two of those reasons, and in doing so commend it to your reading. First of all, there is Flaubert's style. He himself said that he wanted to write "a book about nothing . . . which would hold itself up by the internal force of its style." While *Madame Bovary* is assuredly not a book about nothing, it is certain that the manner in which it is written is astounding, from the masterful portrayal of unforgettable characters to the beauty of the prose (which is most obvious in the original French, but still present in translations). If you want to experience the beauty of language, read *Madame Bovary*. Second, and more importantly, there's Emma Bovary. She is a captivating person in spite of all her faults, or maybe because of them. Emma is on a search for meaning, and she gets herself into all kinds of trouble on this search. She causes herself much pain and grief, and nothing brings her to that state of fulfillment she is trying to achieve. All of this leads to a tragic ending, one that is not unique to Emma. Indeed, we see it every day all around us and in ourselves. Our own searches for meaning—in relationships, in material possessions, in societal standing, in religion—lead us down a painful dead-end road. Fundamentally, Emma's story constantly reminds us that we will not find ultimate meaning in anything other than God himself.

Yearning
by M. Craig Barnes

Perhaps I like this book so much because Barnes begins one of his chapters by talking about Emma Bovary and her quest for fulfillment. Barnes makes the argument that, in spite of what many Christians believe, God does not want us to be fulfilled; he did not create us for that. God is not out to help us get our lives together; rather, he has saved us from such a pursuit that keeps us constantly running from one relationship to the next, one job to the next, one form of spirituality to the next, all with the hope that "this time we'll get it right" and experience joy. For Barnes, true biblical hope is "that in communing with Christ we discover all the grace we need to live joyful but limited lives. For in communing with God we encounter the mystery of his presence with us. Joy is something we receive, and we receive it only through the strange activity of God." This hope is quite different from that which we often cling to: the hope that God will make our dreams come true. I agree with Barnes that although God does indeed fulfill many of our dreams, that is certainly not his ultimate goal for our lives. What he really wants to do is lead us to worship him, to understand our state of creaturely dependence on him and to cling to him, not to what we want him to give us (which we often confuse with him). In doing so we must abandon the idea that God wants us whole and accept the fact that in this life we will always be yearning–yearning for God–and that's the way it should be.

Jonathan Saylor, Conservatory of Music

Pain: The Gift Nobody Wants
by Paul Brand

Paul Brand's book deals powerfully with a profound topic affecting everyone. I have found this work to be a big influence throughout many decisions in my life. What impressed me most about how the problem of pain was treated was how this led directly to Brand's thoughts regarding pleasure–the desire to not only suppress pain, but seek its opposite. He contends that in our modern society we have so raised the levels of what we consider pleasure that they are ever unreachable. He recalls fondly, as a missionary kid in the wilds of India, the pleasure caused by tasting a fresh strawberry–in a land where strawberries were so rare that even one thin sliver produced an almost passionate ecstasy. Now, living as a retiree in the United States, he laments that he is able to purchase fresh strawberries by the case almost anytime, but the pleasure is nowhere near what he experienced in India. Today, Brand asserts, instead of seeking the sweetness of fruit we seek sugar, and keep raising that bar of "what is sweet" until it is beyond reach. On a related matter, this provides at least one powerful explanation behind the proliferation of drugs: the unrestrained search for pleasure. All of this underscores the gift that pain can be, especially in alerting us to important signals from our bodies. We can be thankful that pain is controllable through modern medicine, but we must beware of where our insatiable quest for pleasure can lead us, and the repercussions of that journey.

A Short History of Music
by Alfred Einstein

Though hardly exhaustive, I love this little book for its noble intent and what it tells us about its author. To attempt a "short" history of music is quite a feat, one that few writers could do well. Yet Einstein is able to pack much into this concise, two-hundred-page treatment. Clearly, various "favorite" moments of music's past might be missing for any particular reader. Nevertheless, the fact that Einstein wrote the work in a few weeks, without reference books, poignantly emphasizes how deeply the subject had permeated his whole being. Einstein was an indefatigable worker who possessed one of the great searching minds in twentieth-century music scholarship. His little book on the huge subject beautifully melds his all-encompassing curiosity with his remarkable, encyclopedic knowledge. In sum, the book not only provides all kinds of valuable information and insights, but, more significantly, it represents the noblest aim of the true scholar–the constant desire to learn and to grow. Ultimately, reading this book will inspire the reader to learn and to grow in musical knowledge, too. It is a great introductory survey for someone who wants to learn more about the history of music.

Music through the Eyes of Faith
by Harold Best

As a student and, eventually, a faculty member at Wheaton College Conservatory of Music under the leadership of Dean Harold Best, I was privileged to hear him articulate many of the ideas from this book throughout my numerous interactions with him over the years. For this book is clearly a "summa"–the grand summation–of Dr. Best's many years of deep, integrative thought concerning music and our journey as Christians who practice music, or as he would put it, "think in, up and about music." His ruminations here remind me somewhat of Leonard Bernstein's famous Norton Lectures at Harvard, in 1973. Both feature a popular thread of discourse running through a complex subject. The ideas are wide-ranging and provocative. While you might disagree with some positions, you will always be stimulated, confronted, and ultimately forced to grapple with important aesthetic and moral issues. Harold is one of the most creative, visionary thinkers I've met. For example, one day, as we were discussing creativity, I'll never forget him cocking his head to one side and saying–almost in passing–"I wonder what it was like to create the first cucumber?" The humorous air surrounding such a question suggests that the questioner, the author of this book, continues on a profoundly creative journey; it is a quest that leads Best to ask probing questions about life in the arts. As he moves forward on his journey, he offers many fascinating answers to his curious questions, as this book demonstrates.

Lindy Scott,
Foreign Languages

Rostros del Protestantismo Latinoamericano (Faces of Latin American Protestantism)
by José Míguez Bonino

In the few years since its publication, this book has already become a classic among Latin American evangelicals. This volume brings together messages originally presented as a series of lectures by José Míguez Bonino, an Argentine Methodist who has played a strategic role in Latin American Protestantism over the last half century. I have been quite disappointed by many authors who have studied Latin American Protestantism. Most books are either overly critical and theologically superficial, if written by members of the secular academy, or they are exceedingly triumphalistic, if penned by Latin American evangelicals. Míguez Bonino refreshingly combines rigorous academic analysis with a depth of theological understanding. In the first four chapters, the author evaluates, respectively, Classical Latin American Protestantism, Evangelical Protestantism, Pentecostalism, and Transplanted Protestantism. Míguez Bonino is exemplary because he ably illustrates the Pauline injunction to "examine everything; hold fast to that which is good; and abstain from evil" (I Thessalonians 5:21-22). For example, he applauds Classical Protestantism's emphasis upon individual freedom, human responsibility within community, and the place of reason within religion. Nevertheless, he recognizes that all too often this same Protestantism has been misused ideologically to defend all types of economic and political injustices. Another virtue of the book is that there is a constant dialogue with Christianity outside of Latin America. This helps non-Latin American readers make connections with their own faith, as well as appreciate the unique contributions that Latin Christians have

READING FOR LIFE | 173

made. Míguez Bonino clearly describes how one strength of Latin American evangelicals (their zealous evangelistic proclamation) has also become a weakness by being falsely identified as the totality of the Christian mission. He then appeals for a more complete presentation of the Gospel that would be faithful to the Scriptures. His commentary hits home for me, and at the same time it inspires me onward in the faith.

Paulo Freire:
Una Pedagogía Latinoamericana
by Samuel Escobar

Paulo Freire was clearly the most influential Latin American educator of the twentieth century. This Brazilian's books, especially *Pedagogy of the Oppressed* and *Education for Critical Consciousness*, have had a powerful impact upon literally millions of teachers around the globe, including me. Nevertheless, I was quite frustrated during my sixteen years of ministry in Latin America to see how evangelicals largely ignored Freire and his message. In this book, Samuel Escobar, the well known Peruvian missiologist, provides a great service to the evangelical community by analyzing the life and pedagogy of Freire through the lens of Scripture. Before his death, Freire affirmed that Escobar had written "one of the most complete and accurate interpretations . . . [he] has penetrated my mind . . . even when he criticizes me." Escobar is at his best when he analyzes the anthropology implicit in Freire's pedagogy, according to Scripture. Humanity, for Freire (and for the Bible), is finite, yet we are able to reflect upon our finiteness, which in turn allows us a certain degree of existential freedom to shape our own destiny. In addition to our limitations, we are also morally flawed, in Freire's terms, by personal and structural selfishness. Although Escobar critiques Freire for his overly optimistic view of human nature, he also points out that in some of his writings Freire mentions the need for a "paschal conversion." Such a conversion would produce a necessary and genuine love because "the person who is incapable of loving imperfect human beings is unable to educate them." Escobar then urges us to take the best of Freire's pedagogy and bring it to maturity with a more explicit recognition of human frailty and of the salvific power of Jesus of Nazareth. If Christian communities take seriously this charge, and I think they should, then we will witness "a new liberating education for Latin America."

Tracy Scott, Psychology

Always in Pursuit: Fresh American Perspectives
by Stanley Crouch

Contemporary essayist Stanley Crouch is intellectually mirthful, and a calculated surgeon on the subject of America's psyche. This book is a collection of his best work from 1995 to 1997. In *Always in Pursuit* he discusses the sinister nature of the media and politics, considering their characteristically injudicious effect on the American condition overall. For example, Crouch's epilogue on the O. J. Simpson trial and "The King of Pop," Michael Jackson, is classic in its analysis of the perspicacious nature of the American culture. Crouch is brilliant in his ability to transcend typical American thought and media hype, challenging us with new ideas and insights. I truly gained a greater insight and awareness of the American promise. No other critic offers such a straightforward, even frank, writing style. *Always in Pursuit* is mandatory for anyone interested in dissecting America's true condition.

Black Leadership:
Four Great American Leaders
and the Struggle for Civil Rights
by Manning Marable

This landmark work by historian Manning Marable explores the contributions of economics, politics, and spirituality as they have encouraged the persecution of African Americans. Specifically, he looks at the struggles of Booker T. Washington, Louis Farrakhan, Harold Washington, and W. E. B. DuBois, presenting each Black leader's perspective. Marable's discussion regarding the rhetoric of these leaders is insightfully pregnant, giving a new birth of understanding each time I read it. While reading *Black Leadership*, I experienced a series of emotional quickenings, from feelings of agony to feelings of cautious optimism. This was particularly true when I read Marable's accounts of the prophetic essays of W. E. B. DuBois–noticeably, DuBois' compelling critical analysis of Christians and their insalubrious relationship and furtherance of the mistreatment of Blacks. This is a "must read" for any skeptic interested in knowing why African Americans are historically inauspicious about making genuine improvement in ethnic relationships.

Alan A. Seaman,
Missions and Intercultural Studies

The Memory Palace of Matteo Ricci
by Jonathan Spence

When I went to China as an English instructor in the 1980s, I became fascinated with the history of this immense, enigmatic culture. I was also faced with a practical question: How could I, as a Christian from the West, relate to the Chinese intellectuals I was serving? My search for answers to this question led me to the Yale historian Jonathan Spence, whose biography of the sixteenth-century Jesuit missionary Matteo Ricci is a masterpiece of historical writing. Matteo Ricci was a scholarly missionary who offered the Chinese useful European technologies, such as maps and clocks and scientific texts, while he was becoming deeply acculturated to the patterns of life in China. One of these technologies was a mnemonic device called the "memory palace," which Ricci used to learn the Chinese language and which he taught to Chinese scholars to help them prepare for their arduous civil service examinations. In structuring this biography, Spence recreates the memory palace, moving the reader through a series of rooms and images to tell the story of Ricci's life and ministry. The story ends with Ricci's dramatic entry into a real palace—the Forbidden City in Beijing—as his missionary pilgrimage leads him to an audience with the court of the Ming Dynasty Emperor. Several years ago, as I wandered the grounds of the Forbidden City, I recalled the images in this marvelous biography and realized that the insights from Ricci's life had been added to the architecture of my own memories.

The Reader, The Text, The Poem
by Louise Rosenblatt

For most of my life I have been an avid reader, but before encountering this book I gave little thought to the actual process of reading. Rosenblatt's "transactional" theory of reading is a thoughtful, moderate introduction to thinking about the dynamics of the reading itself. Near the beginning of her career in the 1930s, with the publication of *Literature as Exploration*, Rosenblatt became one of the first critics to examine texts from the vantage point of the reader's experiences. By the Seventies she had been joined by a chorus of "reader-response" critics, some of whom viewed the interpretation of texts as purely subjective and relativistic. But Rosenblatt avoids this extreme by acknowledging the stable character of the text and examining the reading process as a transaction between reader and text. This transaction is described as a lived-through event–the "poem"–which arises from each encounter between the reader and a text. Rosenblatt also coins some useful terms, such as the distinction between "efferent" reading (reading to draw information out of the text) and "aesthetic" reading (reading to create an experience). In our schooling, so many of us have suffered from being forced to read wonderful aesthetic texts, such as novels, in an efferent way– simply to answer the study questions, perhaps, or to pass a test. Rosenblatt's ideas have encouraged me to avoid this mistake as a teacher and, on a personal level, to value more deeply the daily experience of reading Scripture–an experience in which the Holy Spirit is part of the transaction.

Kent W. Seibert,
Business and Economics

The Clashing Worlds of Economics and Faith
by James Halteman

Far too many well-meaning Christians are remarkably ignorant about a subject that affects their daily lives and about which the Bible speaks volumes: economics. Halteman's book does a superb job of simultaneously explaining basic economic concepts and challenging those who already understand the basics to think about economics in new ways. It also provides a systematic, scripturally grounded, and practical model of Christian economics. Halteman's book provides a solid understanding of the differences between pre- and post-industrial society when interpreting biblical passages on economic issues. Such an understanding helps the reader distinguish, for example, between wealth as hoarding for future consumption (which Scripture condemns) and wealth as a form of productive capital (which Scripture does not address). Two of the more radical aspects of Halteman's model reflect its Anabaptist roots: 1) the community of faith (or, local church), not the individual, should be the primary unit of economic decision making; and 2) believers will be most effective as agents of salt and light in the world by modeling an alternative economic lifestyle that reflects Kingdom values. This book has influenced me the most by clarifying the major points of harmony and disharmony between economics and Christianity, and by challenging me in specific ways to submit this important area of my life to God. Furthermore, it appropriately makes claims on the reader's pocketbook, not just the reader's intellect.

The Best Christmas Pageant Ever
by Barbara Robinson

What must it be like to hear the Christmas story for the very first time? What would it have been like to have actually been at the birth of the savior of the world? Predictable and antiseptic answers to these questions are not presented in this book. A friend first read this book aloud to me during Advent, and my wife and I have enjoyed reading it to our children. Using a style that sounds a bit like Garrison Keillor and a bit like Saint Luke, Robinson simultaneously entertains, inspires, and perhaps even shocks her readers. Through the eyes of a child, she describes a Christmas pageant where everything goes wrong and, as a consequence, everything turns out right. The Herdmans, a clan of unchurched, undisciplined, and downright nasty kids, infiltrate the annual church Christmas pageant and bully themselves into the lead roles. Needless to say, the pageant is unlike any before. But its imperfections end up being a better reflection of the imperfect conditions surrounding Jesus' actual birth. And even the Herdman kids ultimately succumb to the wonder of the event. Although written as a children's story, Robinson's tale is equally appealing to adults. More significant than making me smile and laugh, this book has helped me appreciate the mystery and the mundane, the human and the divine, and the fear and the joy of the very first Christmas.

A Severe Mercy
by Sheldon Vanauken

One often hears of books that the reader cannot put down until the book is finished. This was one of those books for me (and for several of the people to whom I have given it). It is a book I have reread several times. Vanauken shares three deeply personal experiences of his early adulthood that shaped his life for now and for eternity. He does this in a richly descriptive and poetic story-telling style that is also appropriately laced with occasional, rigorous, left-brained logic. The three experiences include his idyllic relationship with his wife, his intellectual struggles with doubt and disbelief on his journey toward eventually embracing Christianity, and the emotional and spiritual suffering of losing his wife to an early death. The book is often cited for including letters by C. S. Lewis to Vanauken, which are not published elsewhere and which derive from a friendship between the two men. But for me the value of the book is in the openness and depth with which Vanauken struggles with issues so clearly at the core of human existence. The book stimulated significant spiritual, intellectual, and emotional discussion between my wife and me when we first read it, shortly after our marriage. For anyone who has ever embraced romantic love, undertaken an intellectually rigorous spiritual quest, or suffered grief and loss, this book will resonate profoundly. I have given it to Christians and non-Christians alike, with equally positive response.

David Setran,
Christian Formation and Ministry

The Call
by Os Guiness

An astute social critic, Os Guinness has always challenged me—through such works as *No God But God* and *The American Hour*—to consider Western cultural dynamics from the perspective of the biblical worldview. In *The Call*, however, Guinness explores these dynamics at a deeply personal level, constructing a sophisticated picture of faithful Christian integrity and calling in the modern world. Given to me at a time when I was struggling mightily to weave together belief and behavior in a university context, Guinness skillfully diagnosed a number of the maladies that impeded my spiritual growth. For example, he speaks vehemently against the sacred/secular and public/private dualisms that inevitably constrict the scope of our Christian calling to certain "spiritual" domains. He also speaks to the difficulty of living *coram deo* ('before the heart of God') when our lives are "other-directed," informed by the "roving radars" and "Gallup Polls" that define personal actions in light of what others expect or desire. In a modern world characterized by choice and self-actualization, Guinness calls us to live a life marked by singleness of purpose rather than fragmentation, and responsibility rather than self-absorption. Carefully weaving together biblical, historical, and literary illustrations, Guinness continues to show me that all of life, "everyone, everywhere, everything," must be claimed for Kingdom purposes and the glory of the "Audience of One."

Desiring God: Meditations of a Christian Hedonist
by John Piper

Recommended to me when I first entered graduate school, Piper's book initiated a significant paradigm shift in my life and thought. Standing on the shoulders of such luminaries as Blaise Pascal, Jonathan Edwards, and C. S. Lewis, Piper skillfully articulates a position that affirms the essential goodness of desire. In fact, with Lewis, he contends that our chief flaw is not desire but rather desire wrongly directed toward objects other than God. Struggling myself with a "behavior modification" approach to Christian faith that rejected desire as sinful, I followed Piper's lead to examine the parable of the treasure buried in the field (Matthew 13). I slowly began to realize that faith implied the creation of a "new taste" in which Christ became a "treasure chest of holy joy." The battle against sin now included not only mortification but also the replacement of a superior pleasure that blunted sin's power. Evangelism became a natural outflow since I quite naturally wanted others to revere that which I admired. To say that Piper's work is thorough would be an understatement. His numerous citations, biblical and historical, reveal that this theme is all pervasive, not only throughout Scripture, but also throughout the history of the Church. Establishing worship as our "chief end," Piper's book continues to push me toward a life lived for the glory of God, in whose presence is "fullness of joy" (Ps. 16:11).

Clint Shaffer,
Foreign Languages

Orthodoxy
by G. K. Chesterton

Imagine catching the eye of a friend on some solemn occasion, instantly recalling with her an inside joke or a shared running gag. Picture yourself turning red, shaking with silent laughter, emitting odd little noises that are barely suppressed giggles, and finally losing your composure and guffawing aloud. Then imagine that everyone else in the room–in fact, everyone and everything in the cosmos–is in on the joke. No one is offended and no one looks on disapprovingly. Instead, they join in the laughter, for this is a punch line that never gets old. Then imagine that the joke is actually a remembrance: that, against all hope and logic, contrary to all appearances of an endlessly silent universe, God has, in the glorious words of the first chapter of Hebrews, "in these last days spoken unto us by his Son," and his words are love, mercy, life, and joy. This imagined scene, I think, offers at least a hint of what G. K. Chesterton is about in *Orthodoxy*. His exploration of the Christian faith not only displays a consummate wit (in every sense of the word), but also suggests to the reader that the author's delight in his subject somehow mirrors the pleasure God takes in the work of creation and the bestowal of grace. It is altogether fitting that belief in such a God should be fun, and even in times of doubt or grief, Chesterton's little book serves as a reminder to me that joy has the last word.

Christ the Tiger
by Thomas Howard

In an epilogue written twelve years after the first edition of *Christ the Tiger*, Thomas Howard writes, "Who can unscramble all the tangle of self-dramatization, and self-defense, and blinkered vision, and timidity . . . that bedevils a man's efforts to say something about his experience?" The answer, of course, is no one. And, indeed, certain aspects of this spiritual autobiography from the late sixties may alienate some readers, and the author's sometimes predictable rebellions, crises, and choices may tempt one to toss the book aside with a dismissive, "Get a life!" Getting a life is, however, precisely what the book chronicles, as I realized when I read first it. *Christ the Tiger* is not just about a young man from a conservative evangelical home trying to come to terms with his religious tradition and the world. Rather, it is about the Jesus whom he meets, the Christ who judges his every word and motive and yet shows him the way to an existence in which he can exult without shame. Howard speaks with candor and compassion to anyone who has faced challenges to traditionalistic certitudes, or who has sought freedom by abandoning all commitments. Rejecting the choice between tame faith and unbridled liberty, he instead brings us face to face with the living Son of God, who "tore our secularist schemes to ribbons by announcing doom and our religious schemes to tatters by announcing love."

Joel Sheesley,
Art

Mystery and Manners
by Flannery O'Connor

"The novelist is required to open his eyes on the world around him and look." O'Connor makes so many references to seeing, in this collection of essays about writing, that as a visual artist I thought it was written for me. Perhaps because I have taught for so long in a college where the mind is so highly prized, it was a wonderful relief for me to read this writer whose process of making art begins not with the contents of the mind, but with the world. More than the mind of the artist, O'Connor is interested in his manners, in the concrete nature of his habit of art. Art and art making are, for Flannery O'Connor, incarnational; and that means the mystery of each is discoverable at the point where one can see it operating in people and things. These tangible realities are the true subjects of the artist, be he a writer or a painter. If this news is balancing news to the Christian world, which has for so long favored the abstract and spiritual side of things, it is even better news to Christian visual artists who sometimes feel obliged to illustrate such an ethereal Christian world. With great wit, insight, and variety, Flannery O'Connor makes her incarnational point over and over until a reader might actually begin to believe it. I've been reading through this book once a year for years; it's a persuasion I can't get enough of.

Michael Stauffer, Communication

Free Play: The Power of Improvisation in Life and the Arts
by Stephen Nachmanovitch

As Christian teachers, we are constantly motivated to find new ways of effectively educating the whole person. Nachmanovitch addresses the qualities of the whole person that we hold most dear. Far more than mere self-help, this book is readily applicable to both the rigorous work of academic investigation and the creative process of exploration. Nachmanovitch fully recognizes the inherent tension between these two, yet he is able to weave a tapestry from them that is richer for the diversity resulting from trying to seek a balance between technique and elegance in association with freedom and play. In mentoring the life-long learner, he emphasizes the importance of immersing the learner in the *process* rather than focusing on the ultimate *product*. Seeking a way to ask the right questions is far more important than finding correct answers; it's all about celebrating life as it is now, rather than waiting for life to arrive in some perfect form. As we say in theater, "Life ain't no dress rehearsal." The requisite energy needed to live our lives fully, robustly, comes from an acute and sensitive awareness of being in the moment, ready to grapple with the surprises that inevitably present themselves, as well as the happy accidents that cannot be passed over on the way to the goal. I consider it such a blessing to be able to use this book in class. The discussions with students that have been stimulated by this book, both in and outside the classroom, have been among the most engaging talks I have ever had.

Alva Steffler,
Art

Guilt and Grace
by Paul Tournier

A single reading of a book is about all I ever do. An exception to this is Paul Tournier's book *Guilt and Grace*, which I have read on numerous occasions. While attending seminary, I had a friend who first recommended that I read this helpful book. What a gift of grace it has been to me ever since. In turn, I have shared Tournier's writing with many friends, students, and family members. The first part of the book, "The Extent of Guilt," was right on target in helping me to identify specific "guilt-trips" in my Christian walk, a walk that is often weighted down with the excess baggage of various kinds of guilt, some true and some false. Learning how to deal differently with each kind of guilt has had a most liberating influence on my life. Tournier approaches his subject as a practicing Christian psychiatrist. In the last section of the book, his wise application of theological truths to problems of guilt highlights the grace of God available to all believers, granted through divine forgiveness.

C. Samuel Storms, Biblical and Theological Studies

Desiring God: Meditations of a Christian Hedonist
by John Piper

I refer to this book as a desert island classic. By stating this I mean that if I were stranded on a desert island and had to select two or three books to take with me, *Desiring God* would most assuredly be one of them. Reading Piper's book was truly life–changing, for it awakened in me the stunning realization that I am a hedonist. I am, at the core of my being, driven by the pursuit of pleasure. I am, in fact, more than a hedonist: I am a *Christian* hedonist. That means that the pleasure I seek is all that God is for me in Jesus Christ. Piper takes this simple but controversial notion and applies it across the board to the Christian life. How we view money, marriage, worship, prayer, suffering, and a host of other issues should be filtered through the grid of glorifying God by seeking our gladness in Him, argues Piper. Hard questions are answered and a truly biblical philosophy of life is outlined in this remarkable book. Anyone interested in digging deeply into the essence of human motivation and how it relates to the glory of God should consult this excellent work.

Civility:
Manners, Morals, and the
Etiquette of Democracy
by Stephen L. Carter

I have yet to read anything written by Stephen L. Carter, Professor of Law at Yale University Law School, that I have not felt excited about recommending to others. I first encountered Carter and his writings while doing research in preparation for a course on ethics. This book, in particular, has profoundly influenced my thinking. In it, Carter considers how fundamental virtues are critical not only to individual maturation, but also to the welfare of society as a whole. It is precisely the loss of personal integrity and the demise of civility that account, in large measure, for the unraveling of the moral fabric in our world today. Challenging the notion that bad manners are equivalent with self-expressive "rights," Carter decries incivility. Furthermore, he calls for resolving conflict through dialogue. Writing as a Christian with the clarity and knowledge of a keen legal expert, Carter compels his readers to think deeply about matters that affect us all.

William M. Struthers,
Psychology

The Seven Laws of the Learner
by Bruce Wilkinson

Put very simply, Bruce Wilkinson's *The Seven Laws of the Learner* changed my entire philosophy of teaching. At a time when I was struggling with what my role was as an educator, this challenging and thought-provoking book forced me to radically redefine what I was doing and how I was doing it. Wilkinson's laws provide a blueprint which helps the teacher determine what is being taught, how it is being taught, and who is being taught. The laws of the learner place the responsibility of education on the teacher and offer maxims and practical examples set in a Christian context. As I read the book, I was struck by how much influence a teacher can have on the student. Focusing on students and their relationship to Christ, the book made me realize that my purpose as a teacher should be to engage my students in a relationship which incorporates the subject matter into their walk with God. While the material of each discipline is important, the ultimate goal of every teacher is to communicate truth in order to develop the students as disciples of Christ. Wilkinson's examples and personal experiences provide a wonderful framework for all educators, especially those at a Christian liberal arts college.

The Mind of Christ
by T. W. Hunt

Have you ever wondered what it would be like to actually think like Christ? I certainly have, and that is why I decided to read *The Mind of Christ*, by T. W. Hunt. Aside from being an excellent study in the disciplines of maintaining a godly thought life, it gave me a greater appreciation of what Jesus must have gone through as he walked the earth. The first four chapters focus on the qualities and principles which Scripture provides for governing our minds. The remaining chapters are skillfully crafted and reflect on how a Christ-like mind leads to a Christ-like life. Hunt's gracious writing style is much like a walk in the forest with a wise grandfather who kindly shares advice; I found myself reading the entire text in one sitting because its cohesive quality and logical progression. Having a mind like Christ is a daunting task for the Christian. It is, however, a task that we are called to pursue diligently. Having the mind like Jesus' promises both intellectual and spiritual growth. At the same time, it draws us into a deeper understanding of how magnificent and wonderful Christ's thoughts truly are. At a time when I was struggling with how to discipline my thought life, this book became extremely helpful.

Genesis Unbound
by John Sailhamer

Every so often you read a book that causes you to question how much you thought you knew about something. John Sailhamer's *Genesis Unbound* is one of these books. Unlike many books that dissect Genesis 1-2, Sailhamer offers a unique and fresh perspective on the creation account by challenging the assumptions we make when interpreting the first few sentences of the Bible. His thesis of Historical Creationism takes into consideration both the perspective of the author of Genesis and the creation narrative in its proper context with the rest of the Old Testament. His conclusion that "the land" refers to God's preparation of the Promised Land for the Israelites is intriguing, surprising, and convincing. Like most scientists, I have found the creation account to be one of the more captivating parts of the Bible. *Genesis Unbound* enlightens the reader with a new vision toward integration of scientific discoveries with biblical interpretations. Sailhamer provokes the reader into critically analyzing the common interpretations of Genesis while maintaining the integrity of Scripture. For those interested in gaining a deeper understanding of Genesis, this book will undoubtedly challenge you to reevaluate everything you thought you knew about creation.

Erik Thoennes,
Biblical and Theological Studies

Religious Affections:
A Christian's Character Before God
by Jonathan Edwards

In the church, we often tend to move toward extremes. This seems especially the case in what we consider to be true Christian experience. At times empty emotionalism is seen as the ideal expression of true religion; at other times, cold orthodoxy is esteemed. Written in the thick of the Great Awakening, *Religious Affections* addresses this false dichotomy between reason and the affections. Edwards believes that true religion begins with a work of God in the heart, which is based on sound reason that deeply affects the whole person and manifests itself in obedience. When I read this challenging description of true, holistic conversion, I was moved to fully integrate my faith into every aspect of my being, and to have it show itself in my daily life. This book is as relevant today as it was in 1746.

The Curate's Awakening
by George MacDonald

This is a beautifully written story of a young minister, Thomas Wingfold, who goes through the motions of ministry, lacking true personal faith and devotion. He continues like this until the village atheist confronts him with a question that shakes him out of his Christian role-playing: "Tell me, do you really believe one word of all that?" Unable to honestly answer in the affirmative, Wingfold begins the gut-wrenching process of deciding if he really does believe the claims of Christ. He goes through this journey with the help of a deformed, asthmatic dwarf who is the most godly, yet neglected, member of the community. Macdonald gives us a perceptive look at authentic faith as opposed to empty pharisaical religiosity. This story caused me to reexamine the authenticity of my own faith and recommit to the process of working out my salvation with fear and trembling.

Whoredom:
God's Unfaithful Wife in Biblical Theology
by Raymond C. Ortlund Jr.

Since reading this book, I have often given it as a wedding present. Of course, I do my best to explain why I am giving such an offensively titled book as a gift. My explanation is based on the crucial importance that the theme of this book has for the sober reality of two becoming one flesh. Ortlund traces the theme of spiritual adultery throughout the Bible. The marriage metaphor at the center of God's covenant relationship with his people is the backdrop of God's jealous, angry reaction to their infidelity. God cannot remain ambivalent toward his bride—the Church—when it commits adultery. At the heart of God's pursuit of his straying lover is redemption. Reading this book impressed upon me anew the deeply intimate nature of my relationship with God and my wife. It also highlighted again the metaphorical sacred dignity of human sexuality.

Jeff Thompson, Art

The Mind of the Maker
by Dorothy Sayers

At the time that I read this book, I needed a reason to continue making artwork. By exploring the creative nature of God, Sayers provided me with several parallels between the work of God and the work of an artist that related to *why* someone would be an artist and *how* someone would do the work of an artist. What Sayers' writing did was help me to evaluate the reasons for doing what I do, especially in light of the messages of our culture; it also made me reexamine my intentions in light of God's reasons for creatively entering the world. In reading Sayers' description of God's reasons for the Incarnation, all other reasons for *doing* seem to pale in comparison. God clarified who He was through His Incarnation, and it makes sense to me that we, as artists, need to clarify who we are by making "incarnations" of the invisible, too. So, this is one important parallel that Sayers examines, which gave me the freedom not to need further justification for me *to be* as an artist–just as God needed no justification *to be*. Furthermore, in addition to *why* someone would be an artist, Sayers explains *how* to be an artist. She affirms the nature of allowing a work to grow within you, letting it take its necessary form without imposing on it an outside will; then the artwork has, in a sense, a will of its own. And here she parallels the free will of God's creatures with the creative will of the artist's work. Sayers' views about the creative process, on this matter, freed me to create things, over the next twenty years, without feeling the need to fix them, or change them, or mold them according to the dictates of theological correctness; instead, I tried to let my works of art simply be good works that reflected me as a human being. There was no need of attaining some manipulated or falsified presentation of what I thought would be acceptable. This is another one of Sayers' parallels, showing how God allowed His creation to have a free will, letting it make turns–even indirections–that were not according to His best judgement or His intended end for His creation. Likewise, according to Sayers, I can make my art. I have the liberty to make pieces that are not "the last word" or "the final presentation" of my most pious thoughts, but are the pieces of free expression–of a life. Lastly, Sayers has a chapter on problem solving, which showed me that problems are allowed to remain in the world, in part, as paradoxes, and in part, as an affirmation of our being in relation to a mysterious God. One does not have to end up solving all the problems of the world–to reduce everything to a mathematical formula or explanation. In fact, Sayers emphasizes that such an attempt would not be a fair expression of the way the universe is formed . . . in mystery. To believe that everything has, like a puzzle, its perfect place, or to believe that every puzzle piece and place can be known and articulated by humans, is not in keeping with our limited state of being or the complexity of the world.

Annette Tomal,
Business and Economics

On Behalf of God:
A Christian Ethic in Biology
by Bruce R. Reichenbach and V. Elving Anderson

This informative and thought-provoking book has given me a greater understanding of, and appreciation for, the complexity of many moral issues–issues that often are reduced to simplistic answers preached from many evangelical pulpits. Writing for a general audience, the authors (a biologist and a philosopher) have developed a biblical paradigm of stewardship that identifies three primary functions of Christian stewardship towards the Creator and His creation: to fill, to subdue, and to care for the earth. They then apply that paradigm in analyzing, evaluating, and exploring several moral issues arising out of the field of biology. These moral issues include the environment, human sexuality, assisted reproductive methods, the human genome, and moral responsibility pertaining to genetics. Rather than pronouncing "absolute truth" on any of these moral issues, the authors provide an intellectual and ethical framework, along with background, by which to conduct a serious debate regarding these issues.

Peter Walhout, Chemistry

Beginning to Pray
by Anthony Bloom

This short book, written in 1970 by an Orthodox Archbishop, sparked my own lethargic spiritual life during graduate school by sharpening my understanding of the discipline of prayer. Bloom's refreshing, honest examination of prayer stresses the focus of one's thoughts during prayer, the choice of words used in prayer, and one's attitude towards time. The first chapter, provocatively titled "The Absence of God," describes how our initial feeble attempts at prayer are typically met with an acute awareness of God's apparent absence. Because we are in a personal relationship with God, we must not expect to mechanically draw God into a prayerful encounter unilaterally, as we would an idol. God only chooses to meet us when we are ready for such an encounter, because "a meeting face to face with God is always a moment of judgement for us." The first steps of prayer, then, are to look around for God, to not immediately find Him, and then to earnestly ask "Where is the door and how does one knock at it?" The rest of the book, with the aid of clear writing and poignant examples, helps the reader find the door and learn to knock.

Terri S. Watson, Psychology

An IVP Series on Gender and Singleness:

Women at the Crossroads: A Path Beyond Feminism and Traditionalism
by Kari Torjesen Malcolm

Men at the Crossroads: Beyond Traditional Roles and Modern Options
by Jack Balswick

Singles at the Crossroads: A Fresh Perspective on Christian Singleness
by Albert Y. Hsu

InterVarsity Press has produced a series of thoughtful books on gender and family issues that have been formative in my personal and professional growth over the past sixteen years. Designed to provide a fresh perspective on our cherished traditional notions, this collection of publications challenges Christians to explore the influence of contemporary culture on the biblical values that are central to our lives as singles, couples, and families. I first experienced the impact of these books through reading *Women at the Crossroads* as a Christian undergraduate. At the time I was struggling to understand how my gender actually fit in with God's call to serve Him vocationally. Since then, few publications have shaped my thinking on gender and family issues as have this book and the two follow-up books, *Men at the Crossroads* and *Singles at the Crossroads*. These, along with the books reviewed below, provide an extremely valuable resource for Christians who seek to wrestle with the complexities of how our primary commitment to Christ and His Kingdom will necessarily affect gender and family relations.

Gender and Grace:
Love, Work, and Parenting
in a Changing World
by Mary Stewart Van Leeuwen

Writing from the perspective of a psychologist and Reformed Christian thinker, Van Leeuwan has crafted an eminently readable and intellectually sophisticated text exploring the impact of gender on our spiritual, vocational, and family lives. *Gender and Grace* provides an excellent overview of theological, sociological, and biological perspectives on gender which will answer many of the thoughtful Christian's questions regarding the similarities and differences between the sexes. Some readers may choose to skim the chapters detailing biological perspectives and focus on the "applied" chapters outlining the implications of gender issues for vocation and family. Van Leeuwan offers a taste of how an egalitarian view of gender relations impacts a variety of important issues including parenting, marriage, Christian vocation, and sexuality. Along the way, she never loses sight of our primary call as men and women to serve Christ above all else. I recommend this as an important book for both men and women to read and discuss in pursuit of gender reconciliation, which remains a personal interest for me.

Families at the Crossroads: Beyond Traditional and Modern Options
by Rodney Clapp

Families at the Crossroads is a "must read" for the Christian who longs to understand how biblical perspectives can inform and guide families in the midst of contemporary cultural pressures. I came across this book early in my teaching career, at a time when my family was becoming increasingly challenged by such pressures as our children entered school. Clapp convincingly charges that Christian families have adopted the Western cultural values of capitalism, consumerism, and exclusiveness to the detriment of the church and family. Making an important distinction between the "traditional" concept of the family from the early nineteenth century and the biblical perspectives on the family from the Old and New Testaments, Clapp focuses our attention on the areas where contemporary Christian views of the family miss the mark. He provides an important corrective to modern cultural perspectives by reminding us that the Church, not the family, is God's most important earthly institution. In doing so, Clapp provides a challenge for Christian families to become a "mission base" where children, singles, and strangers are welcomed and cared for with genuine compassion. While the specific solutions as outlined by Clapp may not provide "the answers" for all Christian families, the value of this book lies in its challenge to sincere Christians to evaluate the ways in which both "tradition" and "contemporary culture" can interfere with our service to Christ. *Families at the Crossroads* confronts readers, prompting them to live lives more thoughtfully consistent with biblical values, in service to the church, the community, and the family.

William R. Wharton, Physics

Quarks, Chaos, and Christianity
by John Polkinghorne

John Polkinghorne, physicist and Anglican priest, is a leader and prolific writer in the dialogue between science and religion. This book (as well as the book that follows) represents the briefer works of the many excellent books that Polkinghorne has published. Providing a broad introduction to many of the important issues pertaining to the relationship between God and our universe, this book considers the following topics: evidence for design; the question of evil; the mystery of consciousness; and many issues relating to causality and the ways God may interact with His creation, primarily within the laws of nature. Near the end of the book Polkinghorne has a chapter on miracles, in which he affirms the physical resurrection of Christ; this chapter was particularly striking to me as a believer. The last chapter is devoted to the belief in a destiny beyond death, not just for us, but eventually for the whole universe—another fascinating chapter. However, the main thrust of Polkinghorne's message is to present a harmony between science and religion, an argument that the book demonstrates skillfully.

Belief in God in an Age of Science
by John Polkinghorne

I had the privilege of working closely with Polkinghorne during a five-week Christian Scholar's seminar at the time this book was first published. He is a humble, generous man who provided deep insight into the projects that each of us was working on. This, the second of his two shorter books, focuses more on the nature of science and religion, examining the interplay between them and emphasizing their compatibility. For example, the author shows parallels between the historical effort of science to understand the dual wave/particle nature of light and the early church's effort to understand the dual God/man nature of Christ. After reading this book I concluded that Polkinghorne, a man of deep Christian conviction and prayer, is an enjoyable writer to read. Through his judicious choice of words, he is able to economically bring issues to the forefront. Although Polkinghorne is not a theologian, he has a good, broad grasp of many theologians' work and is skilled at summarizing, comparing, and contrasting other peoples' beliefs and ideas. My familiarity with the writer makes his work all the more significant and easy to recommend.

Paul Wiens,
Conservatory of Music

Guns, Germs, and Steel
by Jared Diamond

This book's central investigation focuses on the causes of the development of various cultures during the last 13,000 years and it seeks to debunk the common view that certain races have advanced principally due to their inherent superiority. The topic and the author's ideas are thought provoking and ground-breaking, even when the writing is not always spellbinding. Certainly the author's grasp of anthropology, behavioral ecology, linguistics, epidemiology, archeology, and the history of technology proves to be impressive. In the chapter entitled "Necessity's Mother," which touched my creative soul and drove me back for repeated readings, Diamond explains several fascinating things: that invention is the mother of necessity; that most inventors are not heroes, but simply offer a slightly improved product; that timing is everything; that cultures are disposed to accepting or rejecting new inventions (regardless of their value); that social value and prestige can override economic benefit; and that technology begets more technology. He succeeded in giving me a context for my creative effort, which was informative and comforting.

James C. Wilhoit,
Christian Formation and Ministry

The Celebration of Discipline:
The Path to Spiritual Growth
by Richard Foster

I first read this book in the early eighties. It had been around for a few years, and many people were talking about it. Clearly, Foster celebrates discipline! He seeks to show how the ancient Christian disciplines can bring about a life of freedom and joy. In fact, the book gives a good theological basis for why we should practice the disciplines in our daily life. After a solid introduction, there is a chapter discussing each of the disciplines addressed. Short and well-written, these chapters provide both theory and application. This format proved especially useful to me, since I had previously realized that the evangelical sin-management approach—all too prevalent—was failing to take me to the spiritual level that I was hoping to attain. Foster is certainly not a legalist; what he offers is an invitation. "Here are things you can do if you're interested in freedom and joy," he seems to say to the reader. Then he provides a picture of hope. Do you want to be trapped in anger, and jealousy, and fear, or do you want to experience freedom and joy? Foster does a very good job of providing alternatives—choices for living a better life. In particular, the first chapter gives a very good theoretical foundation for the disciplines, and it is certainly worth reading several times over. Also, keep in mind that the book does not operate in a rigid chronological order, so one could read around and review the disciplines that seem most appealing. This book represents an ideal friend—one who is always there (albeit, on a shelf), ready for the reader to come back to, time and again, for healthy challenge and growth.

The Spirit of the Disciplines
by Dallas Willard

When this book first came out in 1988, it introduced me to an understanding of Jesus' spiritual life, as well as the spiritual disciplines necessary to follow Him. Furthermore, it gave me a better sense of Christ's own spiritual development. At one level, it strikes me that certain chapters in this book were journal articles. Consequently, it is not a book that is guided by one incredible argument, one that persists throughout. Nevertheless, it examines what discipleship is and what purpose lies behind the spiritual disciplines. Writing from a Baptist perspective, Willard expresses his concern that being "born again" has become the essence of being a Christian. He is concerned also that much of the focus on the "what would Jesus do" phenomenon, and a focus on decisions made in a moment in time, supplant a serious consideration of the decisions that Jesus made. In that sense, Willard prepares the reader for a rationale of why one should cultivate the Christian disciplines. It is hard to imagine that a month goes by that I don't refer back to this book in my mind. Yet it affects me differently now, in part because I have sought to put it into practice. With time, there is a greater sense within me that this book rings true. Experientially, I can relate to Willard's insights and can understand that they are indeed valid. As a philosophy professor, Willard provides several aspects that would appeal to someone who has an analytic bent. And for those who are looking at issues of personal discipleship, they will find the book to be as viable a presentation of the Christian disciplines as there is out there. I think the book is really for anyone who wrestles with the question of spiritual regeneration, our being made new, and how discipleship connects to this process. Willard wrestles with the false notion that sees discipleship as something that is optional, and pins it to the mat. A well-written book, it makes the claim that Christians are content knowing Jesus as savior, but aren't as comfortable knowing him as teacher.

Bud Williams,
Kinesiology

Body, Soul and Life Everlasting: Biblical Anthropology and the Monism-Dualism Debate
by John W. Cooper

Can life continue after death? Challenges to our eternality are no more apparent than when those in science state that man is solely material substance. To many scientists, consciousness, mental capacities, and personality emanate entirely from the brain and not from immaterial factors. If this were so, then personal existence would cease forever at death. Christian tradition affirms an eternal existence that allows for more to human nature than material substance. Scripture teaches an intermediate state when the person somehow comes apart between death and bodily resurrection. However, within the Christian tradition there has been debate and confusion over what these immaterial aspects of human nature are and how they are connected to the body. Since it is apparent that the body remains at death, the body and matter have often been denigrated to a lower status. Having struggled with challenges from materialists and within the church as to what is a proper biblical anthropology, I found Coopers' treatment of this subject philosophically, theologically, and scientifically provocative.

The Divine Conspiracy: Rediscovering our Hidden Life in God
by Dallas Willard

Life often becomes mired in the struggles we encounter, and during those times we need to see the bigger picture. Dallas Willard brings Jesus' teachings to life, making them a part of the big picture. As I see it, Willard is like a skilled artist who reveals aspects of reality (ourselves included) that we never have fully seen. He reminds us that we are flesh-and-blood citizens in the kingdom, existing here and now. We are created to count and to have an effect on our kingdom that is "the range of our effective will." Willard challenges us to be more than bar-code Christians and to enter fully into a transformational process toward Christ-likeness. I found his description of the process to be freeing—beginning with love of Jesus and removing automatic patterns of response that work against our engagement in the kingdom of His love. But the most poignant value of this book came from its potential to connect our present life seamlessly with our eternal existence. As believers, we are invited to become apprentices to Jesus and to develop ourselves to the point where we can fully take our place in the ongoing creativity of the universe. *The Divine Conspiracy* is one of those classics that beckons us to reread it again and again.

Redeeming the Time:
A Christian Approach to Work and Leisure
by Leland Ryken

It seems that we tend to worship our work and to become hedonists in our leisure, and both often lead us to feel guilty. Obtaining a proper biblical perspective on work and leisure in a success-oriented, acquisitive society has been a difficult task for me and the students whom I teach. My colleague, Leland Ryken, with a background in Puritan literature, has provided us with fresh insights on leisure, play, and work to counter contemporary cultural thought. His book raises some important questions: If work and leisure are gifts from God to the human race, what is their intended purpose? Are these gifts also mandates? How should our work and leisure be performed for our own pleasure and God's glory? If our time on earth is short, how should we balance our work with our leisure? Will these activities continue into eternity? Ryken's work, written in a readable prose style, has stretched my thinking and impelled me beyond the status quo.

Clifford Williams,
Philosophy

Escape from Evil
by Ernest Becker

Like its companion volume, *The Denial of Death*, this book describes what Becker believes is the mainspring of human activity, namely, the "urge to deny mortality and achieve a heroic self-image." In *Escape from*

Evil, however, Becker also claims that the very pursuit of the heroism that is a means of bolstering the self is the root cause of human evil. His vivid characterizations of this drive and its effects in personal and social affairs captivate the reader; more than that, they cause one to lose one's sense of innocence. After reading Becker, one can scarcely do anything without wondering whether the desire for heroism has motivated it. One benefit from reading this book is that it pushes the reader toward grace—at least that is what it has done for me. Few books have done this more decisively. Becker's theology may not be precise; nevertheless, his plain but passionate prose and his piercing insights have the power to move the reader to a profound, often painful, depth. For example, he writes, "Man needs self-esteem more than anything; he wants to be a cosmic hero, contributing with his energies to nothing less than the greatness and pleasure of the gods themselves. At the same time this risks inflating him to proportions he cannot stand." These prove to be poignant words, and many more await the reader besides.

The Power and the Glory
by Graham Greene

Jonathan Edwards declared that we must wrestle with grace in order to win it. Graham Greene dramatically portrays this truth in this novel about a Mexican priest who struggles with the appearance of piety and with his addiction to alcohol. Becoming an outcast who is pursued by communists in his own country, the "whiskey priest" desperately grasps for salvation. Though he feels unworthy of being a holy man, he determines to act as a priest should act until he is captured. For years after reading Greene's haunting tale, I felt that I had to read it again. When I finally did, I was moved even more than the first time. Rarely do we find such powerful depictions of a human being's most significant striving—for the security of his soul.

Purity of Heart Is To Will One Thing
by Soren Kierkegaard

One cannot read too much of Kierkegaard without wondering whether one can escape inner dividedness. *Purity of Heart* is especially effective in this regard. Kierkegaard delineates the hidden motives we would rather keep hidden, the rewards we surreptitiously pursue, the fear of disapproval we are unknowingly moved by, our egocentric reasons for doing the good, and the half-commitments that undermine our pursuit of the eternal. Along the way, he describes the excuses and deceptions we use to evade the good. The most ruinous evasion of all, he declares, is to hide in a crowd from God. How can we detect our evasions and subterfuges? By the use of cleverness, Kierkegaard states. But, as he also notes, cleverness is a treacherous friend, for it undermines purity of heart as much as it fosters it. The thought may occur to the reader that perhaps it is better to pursue eternity simply, without the continual self-probing Kierkegaard recommends. But this won't do, either, because what we don't know about ourselves will control us. We are left with a tension: we passionately want purity of heart, yet we recognize that most, possibly all, of our motives are mixed or half-hearted. Kierkegaard doesn't tell us how to live with this tension, though the lesson we learn from him is that we certainly must do so.

W. Jay Wood,
Philosophy

The Brothers Karamazov
by Fyodor Dostoyevsky

To say that Fyodor Dostoyevsky is one of the most compelling, psychologically acute masters of characterization ever to write a novel is to state the obvious. Not so obvious is how his acuity allowed him to see the ways our heart and head come together in the knowing process. In contrast to the prevailing model of his day, one that idealized the utterly detached, dispassionate reasoner, Dostoyevsky shows how our successes and failures as knowing agents are bound up with our moral and emotional lives. This truth is vibrantly portrayed through the character Father Zossima, the saintly monk of Dostoyevsky's *The Brothers Karamazov.* Zossima nicely illustrates the vital connection between our moral and intellectual lives. While recounting to his fellow monks the story of his conversion, he emphasizes how his youthful pride blinded him to obvious truths. As a young army officer with all "the polish and courtesy of worldly manners," Zossima became infatuated with a young woman of high social standing, whom he fancied to be equally infatuated with him. After a brief trip away from the woman, he returns to the town where he is stationed only to discover that she has married a local landowner to whom she had long been engaged. And though he had met the woman's fiancé, and the fact of the engagement was widely known, it had completely escaped Zossima's notice. "How was it possible that almost everyone knew, and I alone knew nothing?" Zossima asks. And to his novices he confesses that he had been "blinded by his own merits." Pride so impaired his cognitive faculties that he remained ignorant of what was obvious to everyone else. Father Zossima's story represents only one of several poignant illustrations of humanity that are blended together in this amazing novel.

Crime and Punishment
by Fyodor Dostoyevski

Moral and emotional exploration continues as we encounter Raskolnikov, the nihilist of Dostoyevsky's *Crime and Punishment*. He abandons his philosophical perspective, not as the result of argument, but in response to the powerful love of a woman named Sonya. After Raskolnikov confesses to having murdered a pawnbroker and her sister, Sonya perceives what a wretchedly tormented soul he is, and in compassion moves to embrace and to kiss him, prompting this response: "You're so strange, Sonya—you embrace and kiss me, when I've just told you about that. You're forgetting yourself. . . . A feeling long unfamiliar to him flooded his soul and softened it all at once. He did not resist: two tears rolled from his eyes and hung on his lashes." Raskolnikov does not merely observe Sonya's expression of love; he experiences himself as one who is loved by her. Through his emotional experience, Raskolnikov construes himself as an object of value, a fact his philosophical theory cannot allow. How can it be simultaneously true that the world is without value (the nihilist view) and that he is himself valuable (according to Sonya's love)? Raskolnikov answers this question by allowing his experience to override his philosophical theory; Dostoyevsky's phrase—"he did not resist"–suggests that Raskolnikov might have resolved the tension the other way, by allowing his prior philosophical commitments to undermine his experience. Nevertheless, in Raskolnikov's case, and so often in our own, a change of mind is precipitated by a change of heart. The lesson of this novel (and the previous one) is one for which I, as an epistemologist, will always be grateful to Dostoyevsky.

Ashley Woodiwiss,
Politics and International Relations

Kristin Lavransdatter (1920) and
Master of Hestviken (1925)
by Sigrid Undset

On November 13, 1928, Sigrid Undet was awarded the Nobel Prize for Literature for (in the words of the Prize Committee) her "powerful delineation of medieval life." Both *Kristin Lavransdatter* (a trilogy) and *Master of Hestviken* (a tetralogy) concern themselves with the Christian themes of sin and redemption. But unlike much contemporary Christian writing, Undset's work attempts to chronicle the consequences of sin in its breadth (its effect upon the community), its depth (its deepest grip upon the individual soul), and its historic reach (even down to the second and third generations). Thus, in *Kristin*, Undset details in heartrending fashion how the impetuous passion of Kristin, who breaks her bethrothal to the solid but unspectacular Simon to pursue an illicit relationship with the dashing but irresponsible Erlend, leads to the disruption of all good (personal and public) in her life. Similarly, in *Master*, Undset chronicles the transmission of sin first begotten when Olav (the future Master) and Ingunn, betrothed when both were but children, prematurely consummate their love, thus setting off a series of recriminations, retributions, and revenge that passes on through the generations. So powerful are the Christian themes of sin and (ultimate, but hard-won) redemption present in these works that they led to Undset's own conversion! It was through the writing of *Kristin* that Undset understood her own spiritual neediness. Consequently, she was received into the Church on November 24, 1924. I routinely read these volumes in the penitential seasons of the Church (Advent and

Lent). Undset herself believed *Master* to be the better of the two works. With that I would agree. I am happy to note that *Master* has been re-issued and is now available in a single-volume paperback though Vintage Books.

David Wright, English

A Timbered Choir: The Sabbath Poems 1979-1997
by Wendell Berry

One early spring afternoon during my undergraduate years at Millikin University, a professor demanded that I hop into his old red pickup and ride with him to the University of Illinois for a poetry reading. Once we arrived, Wendell Berry read from his book of Sabbath poems for over an hour. My life as a teacher, poet, and Christian has not been the same since. For, after the reading, during the drive back across the Illinois prairie, I saw the landscape differently, both poetically and spiritually, in ways I've spent the next fifteen years working out. Anyone who picks up Berry's work (whether essays, fiction, or poetry) will be struck by the profound way he weaves his life and writing together. "All the lives this place / has had, I have," says Berry in his poem "History." "I eat / my history day by day . . . / and am combined within the story of this ground." The urge to figure out how one should live responsibly and beautifully in a particular place informs all of Berry's writing; it has changed my own sense of what making poems and being a steward of Creation might involve. Whether it is *A Timbered Choir* or his *Collected Poems*, readers who love God's handiwork, who understand the joys

212 JEFFRY DAVIS, LELAND RYKEN, THOMAS MARTIN

of staying put, or who can laugh at themselves should not miss Wendell Berry's poetry. For such readers he offers an admonition: "every day do something / that won't compute. Love the Lord. / Love the world. Work for nothing. / Take all that you have and be poor. / Love someone who does not deserve it." Readers will find it difficult not to pay just as much heed to this poet's lifetime of digging into the dirt, as well as his digging into language, all, as Berry writes, in order to "practice resurrection."

Reggie Young,
English

The Adventures of Huckleberry Finn
by Mark Twain

Some scholars argue that an authentic American literary tradition began with the anecdotes, stories, and novels of Mark Twain, which are set near the banks of the Mississippi River. Those scholars recognize Twain's *Huck Finn* as the first truly American masterpiece in fiction, a novel that led later writers such as Ernest Hemingway, William Faulkner, and Ralph Ellison to acknowledge its influence on their work. Twain explores the nation's literary frontier by portraying uniquely American subjects in a language that is poetic, despite his heavy use of humor and colloquialisms. I must also confess that no other work influenced my early efforts to write fiction more than this one. I saw so much of Huck in myself as a youth that I once named a semi-autobiographical character "Jim Finn," a name that combines Huck's last name with his slave companion's first name. Ironically, Huck attempts to help Jim reach freedom by traveling *down* the Mississippi River on a raft, farther into slave holding states. Though the novel is flawed–for example, Tom Sawyer literally takes over the last third of the book and throws the narrative into mayhem–the scenes on the river with the boy and slave are among the most captivating in American literature.

Cane
by Jean Toomer

It was the first section of Toomer's book that made me want to explore the possibilities that literature might offer for my life when I was a youth. As naive as it might sound, after reading the first poetic sketch titled "Karintha," I thought I had fallen in love with the title character. Never had I read anything so beautiful, and the beauty of the prose and the poetic refrain that runs through the piece obscured the fact that I, too, was one of those blinded men who would possess this girl–a girl who grows into a woman too soon. Due to the corrupting influences of her environment, growing up in a former slave shanty that was built on the "two room plan" where children were exposed to adult intimacy, Karintha becomes a "ruined" woman. Nevertheless, I still loved this character. It was not until I became a more sophisticated reader that I realized it was not Karintha I loved, as woman or character, but it was the beauty of Toomer's language. Toomer is a complicated but fascinating writer, and *Cane* remains one of my favorite books today.

A Lesson Before Dying
by Ernest Gaines

One of the most interesting aspects of this novel is the attempt of two elderly women, descendants of slaves on a mid-twentieth century plantation, to force the plantation's teacher to help a condemned youth die like a man. Jefferson, the eldest woman's godson, is labeled a "hog" when his own lawyer appeals to the jury for leniency, telling them they would not bother to execute any other dumb beast. Although probably innocent, Jefferson's actual innocence or guilt is of little importance to the plot. The narrative suggests that before Jefferson can accept Christ as his savior, he must accept himself as a man, overcoming his feelings of self-pity and degradation. Even Jefferson admits "He [Christ] didn't die for no hogs." Although Grant, the teacher, abandoned his faith after he went away to college, the women are wise in challenging him to help redeem Jefferson's humanity. His efforts to encourage the condemned man to meet his maker "on two legs and not on all four" help to soften his own heart as he becomes the kind of teacher their community needs him to be.

The Most Influential Books

Books Chosen by More than One Teacher

(In Alphabetical Order by Title)

The Brothers Karamazov
by Fyodor Dostoyevsky

The Celebration of Discipline
by Richard J. Foster

Christ and Culture
by H. Richard Niebuhr

Desiring God
by John Piper

The Divine Comedy
by Dante Alighieri

The Great Divorce
by C. S. Lewis

In the Name of Jesus
by Henri J. M. Nouwen

Man's Search for Meaning
by Viktor E. Frankl

Mere Christianity
by C. S. Lewis

Orthodoxy
by G. K. Chesterton

Pensées
by Blaise Pascal

The Pilgrim's Progress
by John Bunyan

A Room of One's Own
by Virginia Woolf